# PROSPECT
—— THE ——
# SANDLER WAY

# PROSPECT

## — THE —

# SANDLER
# WAY

*A 30-Day Program for Mastering*
*Stress-Free Lead Development*

**PROSPECT THE SANDLER WAY**
*A 30-Day Program for Mastering Stress-Free Lead Development*

ISBN: 978-0-9832614-4-5

Visit us at www.sandler.com to learn more!

*To your future.*

# TABLE OF CONTENTS

# ACKNOWLEDGMENTS

I want to thank the Sandler Home Office team for their vision and support, in particular Yusuf Toropov and Howard Goldstein. My gratitude also goes out to the incredible team at Sandler Training Pittsburgh, Pennsylvania and Charleston, South Carolina. Their commitment, dedication and excellence still amazes me twenty years later. I owe thanks to Jeanne and Lar Rosso—the best parents anyone could have. They taught me the value of hard work and optimism. My children, Jack, Steve, Cait and Joe are also on my thank-you list. They are all so different, and all perfect. And finally, deepest gratitude goes out to my wife, Catherine, who in every situation demonstrates grace, beauty, patience and love.

# FOREWORD

John Rosso has a plan.

Unlike a lot of plans people offer salespeople in regard to prospecting – unlike the plans laid out in other books you may have read on this subject — this plan is a perfect plan. It will work for you, no matter what your product or service is, no matter what industry you sell in, no matter what the economic climate is like, and no matter what the competition is doing. As long as what you do involves creating new relationships with new prospects, John's plan will deliver positive results for you and increase your income ... if you follow it.

This the same plan our company's founder, David H. Sandler, used to build his business from the ground up. It's the same plan Sandler shared with John twenty or so years ago, although you'll notice that John has updated some key elements for the Internet age. It's the same plan I use to drive my own business. *This plan works.* I can vouch for that much personally.

This prospecting plan you'll learn about here doesn't ask you to embarrass yourself, or stress yourself out, or stress the prospect out, or make outlandish claims that mislead people. This plan doesn't leave anything out, and it won't take long at all for you to learn and put into practice. If you've got thirty days, and you're willing to devote them to executing the activities you'll find on the pages that follow, *you will succeed.* That's my personal commitment, and my challenge, to you.

You're holding a perfect prospecting plan in your hands. Read it. Study it. Follow it!

—*Gerry Weinberg, Founder and CEO,*
*Gerry Weinberg & Associates, Inc.*

# ABOUT THIS BOOK

**Prospect the Sandler Way** outlines thirty core principles for mastering stress-free lead development by phone, in accordance with the selling system developed by David H. Sandler. We have updated some of the techniques and made these 30 prospecting principles accessible and viable for 21st century sellers, but the core concepts are those of the Sandler Selling System methodology.

This book will be most effective for yourself and/or your team if you read and implement one principle per day over a period of thirty days. Let one principle sink in for a full 24 hours, and be sure to complete any activities connected with that principle before you try to master the next one.

# INTRODUCTION

## *Can This Marriage Be Saved?*

O nce upon a time, there was an extremely nervous man who showed up on the doorstep of a woman he had never met (or even seen) before. He'd heard good things about her and decided it was time to get married.

He knocked on the door briskly.

She opened the door and saw a stranger with trembling hands and a clenched jaw. Summoning up all his courage, he introduced himself and asked her whether she would marry him, right then and there.

Amused, she looked him over, paused for the briefest moment imaginable, said *no,* and closed the door.

Dejected, he moved to the next house over, made his trembling way up the stairs, and, with his jaw still clenched, knocked on the next door. Supposedly there was a nice woman who lived there, too.

## Are You a Hasty Suitor?

At Sandler Training, which I've had the honor of being part of for the past 20 years, we've worked with hundreds of thousands of salespeople. Most of them were not happy about taking on the responsibility of prospecting. At first, when many of them shared their feelings about prospecting, their behavior reflected something similar to that hasty suitor on the doorstep.

I've even had salespeople tell me that they felt rejected, desperate, and humiliated whenever the dreaded time came for them to pick up the phone and call perfect strangers. This is before they dialed a number!

Most "default" prospecting routines are choked with fear. Is yours?

If so, get ready for some good news.

This book takes a totally different approach to prospecting for professional salespeople—an approach that's far more effective than the "nervous suitor" approach. . . and a lot less scary.

## A Proven System

In terms of identifying actual income opportunities, let's assume that you would prefer to use a system that has been proven to work over one that has not been proven to work. Let's assume you would prefer to use a system that doesn't require you to abandon your self-respect over one that does.

The approach you'll be reading about here has been tested and found to work in virtually every industry that employs salespeople. It comes with a catch, however. **You must be willing to change what you've already gotten used to doing (or perhaps avoiding) when it comes to prospecting for new business.**

In other words, you must be willing to change the patterns you are used to. If you are used to materializing on people's doorsteps (or telephones) with trembling hands and a clenched jaw and then asking them to marry you on the spot, this book will challenge you to try something different and see how it works.

## "Nice to Meet You—Leave Me Alone"

Selling is a lot like dating: a bad first date can leave both sides feeling wary and uncomfortable.

As a consumer, we've all had salespeople call us up on the assumption that we would agree to meet them on the altar and say "I do" within the first five minutes. If you stop to think about it, you'll realize that usually, you didn't respond well when someone called you up and said, in so many words, "Hi, when are we going to get married?"

Stop and think for a moment. What *was* your response?

Did you say, "Great idea—let's go make this happen"?

Or perhaps you were more tempted to say something like, "Gee, I'm really busy right now." Or, "Send me some information." Or, "Call me back in six months."

Let me be very clear: You don't have to get down on one knee in order to be a hasty suitor. In the prospecting sense, "getting married" could mean buying a product or service, or it could mean agreeing to a meeting or some other imminent commitment that moves the salesperson's process forward.

Either way, when you heard that "marriage proposal" from someone who was scared and in a hurry, it's a good bet you weren't always ready to say *yes*.

If this were a real first date, you not only wouldn't marry the person. . . you wouldn't want to see him or her ever again. You'd probably put the person on a stalker (Do Not Call) list!

## A Better Way to Get the "Second Date"

Rest assured that there is a better way to get a "second date." But to take advantage of it, we must be ready to challenge some misconceptions about selling.

For one thing, we have to abandon the idea that memorizing the "right words" ahead of time, and then saying those words verbatim during the first conversation, will get us where we want to go.

That is not what determines the quality of our initial discussions. Memorizing a few pick-up lines is not what makes the difference in the world of dating. And it's not what makes the difference in the world of selling, either.

You may as well know now that this is not a book about snappy sentences you memorize ahead of time. If you came here looking for scripts to simply copy and recite word for word, you won't find them here. . . and you wouldn't be any more effective if you did. I'll give you plenty of ideas for supporting stress-free dialogue during the call. But you will always be responsible for using these ideas to speak like a human being who's communicating with another human being, not like an android who's talking to another android.

When we robotically "stick to the script" during prospecting discussions. . . when we ignore the underlying dynamics of the relationship, we are likely to find ourselves in the same category as that hapless suitor on the doorstep. We will be dismissed as clueless, or arrogant, or abrasive, or disturbingly supersweet or wimpy—no matter what words we have memorized ahead of time.

Why is that? It's because, script or no script, we're tense. And have you noticed that whenever we're tense, prospecting calls tend to go badly? This brings us to a key point: **Success in prospecting is more about *core principles* than it is about memorizing certain words.**

So that's the first key point. You will be learning lots of *core principles* in these pages. It's not all that important that you memorize these principles and be able to recite them in order. What's more important is that you internalize them to the point that you "get" them. Once you "get" the core principle, you won't have to bother yourself about whether or not you've memorized anything. That's the way it is with a lot of things in life, and that's the way it is with prospecting. **Consider focusing on "getting" one principle a day. Don't try to read this book in one sitting. It's okay if you master the prospecting principles, one day at a time, and it's probably better that way.**

One more key point is in order here before we get started.

**Key point number two: When you read "prospecting" here, we're going to assume that means talking to people, either over the telephone or by some other real-time vocal communication device.** Of course, there are a lot of other communication activities we can take part in nowadays—activities that can connect, somehow, to the task of generating revenue and that have nothing to do with talking to people out loud in real time: texts, emails, social media posts. There is nothing wrong with any of these activities. But until you connect with someone voice to voice you're in the world of marketing rather than the world of selling. Marketing is great, but we are focusing on sales prospecting in this book. If you are a fan of social media and interactive communication tools, I think you will be interested to see how those tools can tie into the prospecting process, which is something covered a little later in the book. This book doesn't ask you to ignore the Internet, LinkedIn ®, email, or any of the other great tools that are now at our disposal as professional salespeople, but it does ask you to think of them as a means to an end: a voice-to-voice discussion with a prospect.

**If you think you are ever going to reach a point in your sales career where you *don't* need to talk to people about what you do for a living, think again.** There have been some amazing advances in recent years in the area of personal communication. But no matter how easy, informal, or accessible our communication becomes, we are still going to need to connect to potential buyers on a person-to-person level, and we are still going to have voice-to-voice technology to help us do that. This book has been written on the premise that a good real-time voice-to-voice conversation is, and is going to remain, a primary selling tool in the professional salesperson's arsenal. I am all for using LinkedIn and other social media platforms to support your prospecting. They often provide great information you can use to add that personal touch to a voice-to-voice conversation.

Let's look now at the first, and probably most important, principle for those who want to **prospect the Sandler way.**

# CHAPTER ONE

## *Sandler Prospecting Principle #1: Relax.*

O f course, relaxing during prospecting discussions is, for many of us, much easier said than done. Yet this principle remains an important one. In fact, in a very real sense, relaxing is the governing principle of everything you will learn in this book. Every tool that David Sandler, the founder of our company, ever developed on the topic of prospecting was really designed to help you, as a salesperson, relax and be more effective during these initial discussions.

### YOUR BIGGEST CHALLENGES

Let me ask you a question: Right now, what are the biggest challenges you face when it comes to prospecting? What is it about your current prospecting process that makes you tense up the minute you even think of these things?

When we ask this question during training programs, these are the kinds of answers that come back:

- I get stopped at the gatekeeper.
- People don't return my messages.
- People say they're already happy with what they've got before I even tell them what I'm calling about.
- People tell me to email them something or send information.

Did any of those challenges ring a bell?

Often, salespeople are tempted to assign these kinds of challenges to deficiencies in their calling scripts. They think that, by revising the script, they can make these kinds of problems go away. But we believe that the script you're using is not the problem at all.

In fact, all of the common challenges you just read—getting stopped at the gatekeeper, not having your messages returned, being told that the person is happy already before you say the reason for your call, and being told to send information—have far more to do with us than with our script.

These kinds of challenges are very likely to connect to a certain hard-to-define "something" that the other person hears in our speech patterns. This "something" lies beneath the script and gives the person we're talking to pause. . . and we probably wouldn't even notice it ourselves, unless we listened to a recording of the prospecting conversation and analyzed it very carefully.

This "something" is called a "tell." A tell is a subconscious or semiconscious verbal or nonverbal signal we send to the other person that we are nervous, stressed, fearful, or otherwise insecure about the exchange in which we are involved. These signals, and their accompanying tonalities, are what actually cause the vast ma-

jority of prospective buyers to "bail" on discussions with us. Tells
are the prospecting equivalent of that doorstep suitor's trembling
hands and clenched jaw.

Here's the bad news: To get rid of "tells," we need to do more
than change our script. We actually have to change the way we
think about ourselves.

Here's the good news: David Sandler's selling system makes it
easier to change the way we think about ourselves than we may
have expected.

## UP TO YOU

Don't worry. What follows is not offered as a self-help book.
Helping you in any other area of your life besides prospecting is
simply an added bonus. That's true of the entire Sandler System,
not just the prospecting strategies you'll be reading about here.
The Sandler principles are powerful selling tools and, coinciden-
tally, tools that can help you in your larger life. We only emphasize the improvement in sales performance, which is the proven
outcome we have delivered across all industries. What you do
with these principles in any other area of your life is up to you.

When it comes to prospecting, it's up to you to be yourself.
No one else can do that for you. Most salespeople are incapable of
relaxing and being themselves during prospecting calls. . . and that
means they lose countless opportunities needlessly.

Being yourself is, believe it or not, the biggest prospecting challenge of them all, and the one that, at the end of the day, you're not
going to be able to avoid. Perhaps that doesn't sound like a lofty
enough goal for a book like this. I can assure you, though, that it is
a very ambitious goal. Relaxing and being yourself during a prospecting discussion sounds like it should be relatively easy to do,

but for most people, it proves incredibly difficult in the moment.

To illustrate the real-life dimensions of that challenge, let's look at the single most common complaint that we hear.

## "I Get Stopped at the Gatekeeper"

In my experience, this is nearly universal among salespeople. . . which is absolutely astonishing when you realize that most gate-keepers have a very simple purpose in life, namely, to ask *three simple questions*, all of which we could prepare for ahead of time.

Take a listen. (By the way, the words in italics are the *tells.*)

Gatekeeper: Joe Smith's office; this is Jan speaking.

Salesperson: *Uh. . . yeah. . . I was wondering whether Joe is in?*

Gatekeeper: May I ask who's calling? (That's the first question.)

Salesperson: *Uh. . .* this is Bill.

Gatekeeper: And your company? (That's the second question.)

Salesperson: *Er…* Acme Training.

Gatekeeper: Bill, will he know what this is about? (That's the third question. It may also be phrased as "to what is this in regard?")

Salesperson: *Uh. . . .*

We've all done this. Now we are effectively trapped. We're slipping down the drain. Again, all that's happened is that the gate-keeper has asked three questions that we could have (and should have) predicted ahead of time. . . and prepared for ahead of time!

So what is going on here?

This is not even a conversation. It's a pattern of conditioned responses on both sides. This is Pavlov's dogs all over again. And guess what? The conditioned responses started swinging into action thanks to our *tells,* which we did not "script."

It's what happened *in between the words* that kept us on the doorstep, wringing our hands and staring at a slammed door.

To find out how those "tells" got into that brief, fateful exchange without our meaning them to, to find out what they told the gatekeeper about how the call had to end, and to find out how we can begin the relatively simple process of getting rid of the tells once and for all so we can finally relax and be ourselves during these calls, keep reading.

## The Smell of Fear

You just saw an extremely common crash-and-burn scenario involving an exchange between a salesperson and a receptionist. Now, if you've ever read any other books on prospecting, or taken a prospecting course from someone besides Sandler, you may have expected to see something simple that you could memorize, something that would "fix" this type of obstacle for you by giving you a sequence of "right words" to say. You may have expected some prewritten dialogue that you could simply post on your cubicle, consult, and repeat each and every time you connected with a receptionist. In fact, my guess is that, when you read that I did not plan to build this book around the principle of memorizing such dialogues word for word, and then reciting them to people, you felt just a little let down.

Don't feel that way. Feel relieved.

When it comes to prospecting, memorizing things ahead of time is usually part of the problem, not part of the solution. That's because reality is just too complicated to follow a pre-memorized pattern, especially during a sales discussion. There is a place for familiar phrases and openings that make you feel good about calling people, of course. Before we can talk about that, though, we have to talk about priorities.

The good news is that, if you're looking for help with that call to the receptionist (or with any other call), you can now relax. You're about to get clear on your priorities!

Later on in the book, I will be giving you the guidelines that will allow you to maintain the momentum you need during prospecting discussions, and eventually I will be sharing a sequence of familiar topics that will be authentic to who you are as a person, that will require virtually no effort to deliver, and that will be flexible and adaptable.

But this won't be a "script." It will be you.

## THE SMELL PROBLEM

In order for you to take full advantage of *you* during prospecting calls, we will have to do a little coaching first. We will have to make some commitments to each other. We will have to be willing to change much more than the words you are saying.

We will have to change the way you smell.

No, I am not kidding. When you get right down to it, this is not a script problem. It's a smell problem!

That's because once the receptionist—or anyone else you talk to during the prospecting call—*smells fear* from your side of the conversation, what you have memorized does not matter!

Would you like to know what really happened during that call to the receptionist? Those "tells" ("um," "er," "uh," etc.) sent a powerful signal to that receptionist. Those "tells" told the receptionist that we were uncertain and fearful about the call we were making. The moment we delivered them, we stank of fear.

That smell of fear set off a conditioned response deep within the receptionist's nervous system: *keep this person from getting through.*

That response didn't make the receptionist a bad person; it just made the receptionist someone who was doing her job. That's half of what a good gatekeeper is paid to do, after all: keep the "wrong" people out. The other half of the receptionist's responsibility, the half we'll be making use of in a later chapter, is just as challenging: let the "right" people in! And sometimes that's a tricky business— figuring out who does and doesn't deserve to get through. Over the weeks, months, and years that gatekeeper has been on the job, though, a system of instant classification has proved remarkably helpful and accurate for her. It sounds like this: *people who sound uncertain or fearful over the phone are usually people who need to be kept "out."*

Now let's look at how the receptionist went into "autopilot" mode in direct response to the smell of fear: she started asking questions. These questions almost sounded like a parent questioning a child: Who's calling? What is this regarding? And so on. She has learned to use that tone of voice for one simple reason: it works.

Now, if you stop to think about it, you'll realize that the receptionist's tone of voice is close or maybe even identical to the one your mom or dad may have used years ago to ask you questions like, "Where are you going?" "Why don't you put your coat on?" "When are you going to be back?"

Before you start resenting the receptionist for taking that parental tone with you, consider this: *you told her to take that tone.*

Believe it. In the opening few seconds of that call, those "tells" not only filled little gaps in the conversation but also sent a silent message to the receptionist. They told her you did not consider yourself to be an OK person and were looking for approval, validation, and support from other people in order to *be OK*. That's what set off the smell of fear.

## ARE YOU OK?

Whether they realize it or not, most salespeople do not consider themselves OK and are looking for approval from others. They have failed to internalize a principle that is much, much more important than the words of a script: the sales process is not where you want to get your emotional needs met.

Years ago, when I was beginning to master the Sandler Selling System methodology, I had the honor and the privilege of working directly with David Sandler as my personal instructor. I was still hung up on the idea of memorizing a script that would generate my appointments. I wanted a set of magic words I could say into the telephone. I wanted the words that would reliably deliver the 10 appointments a week that Sandler and I had figured out that I needed. And I felt like I had a great script.

Now, before I had even started calling to set appointments, Sandler had shared a lot of ideas with me about what seemed at the time like touchy-feely stuff. I fast-forwarded over all that mumbo jumbo, finalized my calling script, and started dialing.

A week later, I had to call Sandler and say, "Dave, I've got a problem with my numbers."

He said, "What's that?"

I said, "Well, back in grade school, they told me that you can't divide by zero. So that means I can't tell you how many dials I'm going to have to make in order to get 10 appointments a week. I made 150 dials this week and I got zero appointments. If I had gotten one appointment, I could have told you that it would take me 1,500 dials a week to hit my target. But I've got zero. So I can't tell you anything. Except that I think I'm going to have to change my script."

Like the great teacher he was, Sandler patiently suggested that I might want to think about changing some other things first.

He said that we had something much more important to work on than rewriting my script: I had to change the interpersonal dynamic that was causing me to slip into a black hole on my calls. At some level, I was seeking approval during the call. Without realizing it, I was looking to get my emotional needs met in my prospecting calls. And I was falling into that black hole, over and over again.

No script, he assured me, was going to turn that black-hole dynamic around. I could have had the greatest script in the world, but if the transaction I was engaging in with the people I was calling stayed the same, then the results would be the same, too. If I could understand *myself* and why I was calling people, he promised, I could turn the cycle around. And that had to change first.

Then he started talking about all that touchy-feely stuff all over again. This time, more carefully. What choice did I have? I was batting zero for 150.

Once I actually started paying attention, I began to see areas where I could make some simple changes. What Sandler shared with me during those coaching sessions changed my career—and my life!

If the concepts that David Sandler shared with me could turn around my abysmal numbers, and they did, I know they can turn around your numbers... if you're willing to give them an honest try.

# CHAPTER TWO

*Sandler Prospecting Principle #2:*
*Take Responsibility for Your Beliefs*

Some salespeople—most salespeople, in fact—flinch whenever they reach a certain point in the prospecting call.
The point when they flinch may vary from person to person. The salesperson may think that this flinching is the result of something the prospect has done or failed to do. In fact, though, salespeople flinch when they themselves experience some kind of disconnect. Somehow, they come unglued and seem to disintegrate. What's worse, the prospect can tell they've come unglued. The prospect knows full well that the salesperson is beginning to fall to pieces and that the pieces are beginning to swirl down a deep black hole. To stop the floundering, salespeople must change something important: not their scripts but their *beliefs*.

Beliefs are what we'll be looking at in this chapter.

## WHAT DO YOU BELIEVE?

A belief is something we know to be true based on our own past experience. Sometimes we come to believe some pretty strange things.

Those of us who, for decades, have been training the Sandler System have heard salespeople from every industry you can imagine say something like the following: "CEOs don't want to take my calls."

That's one of their *beliefs* about prospecting. It's based on some kind of personal experience, either something they did or something that someone else told them. As a result, this belief about CEOs is one of the core assumptions that these salespeople bring to prospecting.

There are plenty of salespeople out there who believe this: "CEOs don't want to talk to me; they don't take calls from people like me." But those salespeople didn't say those words, or anything like them, right out loud. It makes no difference. Whether the belief about CEOs is stated explicitly in audible words or left unstated, the end result is the same. The belief ultimately determines the results. Here's how it works:

The person's belief leads to judgments about what *other* people think and believe. (In this case: "CEOs don't want to take my calls.")

Those beliefs and judgments then combine to dictate the salesperson's actions. In the overwhelming majority of cases, a salesperson operating under this belief system will call very few or no CEOs.

This pattern of action leads to a predictable result: the salesperson gets no appointments with CEOs.

Here's the interesting point: Because human beings automatically seek out evidence that confirms their own core assumptions, that result—zero appointments with CEOs—reconfirms the whole cycle and makes it more likely to repeat itself. The salesperson now has—or thinks he has—"proof" that "you can't schedule meetings with CEOs." Those of us who *do* regularly make prospecting calls to CEOs, and who regularly schedule meetings with them, have a different pattern of beliefs, judgments, actions, and outlook.

## THE SELF-FULFILLING PROPHECY

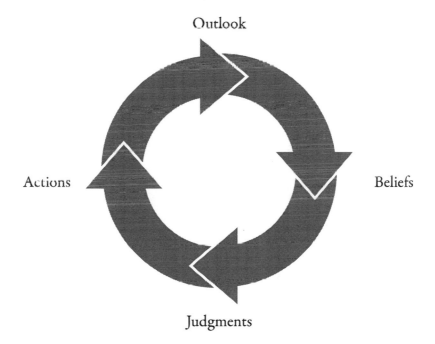

Outlook

Actions

Beliefs

Judgments

Exactly the same dynamic plays out when the belief in question is one that very few salespeople would actually say out loud in public. For instance: "All gatekeepers on earth are out to keep me from getting through to decision makers."

Absurd as it sounds —is it really likely that each and every one of these people wakes up in the morning personally committed to this goal? — this is a common personal belief about selling. Even though it is rarely expressed in words, this belief has a huge effect on people's income and on their performance. Take a look at what happens.

The salesperson's beliefs about gatekeepers as a group lead to a judgment about a particular gatekeeper's intentions. ("Watch out. This gatekeeper is yet another one who is out to make my life miserable.")

Those beliefs and judgments then combine to dictate the salesperson's action. In many cases, he falters during the call as part of a misguided defense reaction, usually a semiconscious "er" or "um" vocalization that sends the gatekeeper a "tell:" *This person is uncertain. Stop the call here.*

The result is that the gatekeeper stops the call and the salesperson doesn't get through. The salesperson now has more "proof" that all gatekeepers are out to keep him or her from getting through to decision makers.

In a minute, you'll learn how to turn around this very common self-reinforcing pattern. What I want you to notice now, though, is that the real challenge isn't anything the gatekeeper says or does. The real challenge is turning around the less-than-useful initial belief that we may have built up and reinforced over a period of years or even decades.

## A Question

For people who actually do manage to break this cycle, what do you think changes first: belief or action?

The answer we typically get from training program participants is "belief." It sounds like the right answer, perhaps because we all want to think we're in conscious control of our beliefs at all times. But we aren't. So that isn't the right answer!

As we've already seen, we human beings are hardwired to look for reasons to *hold on* to existing beliefs, prejudices, and assumptions. As a result, it's extremely difficult to change a belief purely by force of will. If we sit around and wait for our beliefs to change before we start making calls to CEOs, when will we make our first call?

Never!

If we truly want to change the pattern and retire a limiting belief, we have to take action first. We have to make a conscious choice not to let the way we feel control the way we act. We have to use action to change the way we feel. That's often quite difficult. But you know what? Difficult beats impossible any day of the week.

When we finally do take action in opposition to an established active belief like *CEOs don't want to talk to me because they don't take prospecting calls,* we should expect to feel a little weird. Why? Because we are acting 180 degrees from our existing belief system. By definition, we are out of our comfort zone. That's the only way to create new evidence and establish a new belief: to go outside of the comfort zone and create a new personal experience on which to base that belief.

## A Fact of Life

It is a fact of life that people in general, and salespeople in particular, adopt a whole range of beliefs based on past experience. Some of these beliefs support our highest aspirations—others do not. Many of our most powerful beliefs concern what we "know to be true" about ourselves.

Consider the following scenario, which David Sandler was fond of sharing with his students:

You are all alone on a beautiful desert island. There is plenty of food; the weather is great. No predators are threatening you. You have no responsibilities to fulfill, no expectations to meet, and no one to impress or take care of. You have left all your roles behind. The only role you need on this island is you.

So there you are on the island. Using zero for the lowest possible grade, and 10 for the highest possible grade, assign yourself a numerical grade right now. Write the number in the box below. Then write one or two sentences explaining why you chose the number you did.

**YOUR RESPONSE HERE**

_____

_____

_____

_____

_____

_____

_____

_____

_____

**In the next chapter, you will learn about what that number you just wrote meant. Do not move on to the next principle without having completed this exercise.**

# CHAPTER THREE

## *Sandler Prospecting Principle # 3: Identity vs. Role*

**W**hat number did you assign to yourself?

Was it anything other than a 10?

If so, guess what? You are the victim of a misunderstanding.

Someone probably tried to sell you this misunderstanding long ago (it's a very popular item) and for whatever reason, you bought it. Who knows why. Who cares why! When put into words, the misunderstanding sounds like this: "I am not OK."

Now, if someone had asked you to rate yourself as a tap dancer, or a builder of bridges, or an astronaut, or any other job, some number less than 10 might make sense. Those are all roles, and you might consider yourself to be proficient within that role, or less than proficient. But nobody asked you about your role. We asked you about you! Your status as a human being. And as a human being, you really are OK. No matter what anyone else may have convinced you of previously.

As a human being, you deserve a 10 out of 10. Any other score is a misunderstanding.

If that seems like a foreign idea to you, then somebody sold you a bill of goods. If you bought that misunderstanding, yesterday or decades ago, it is now time for you to demand a refund. . . by taking action.

What kind of action do I mean? The kind of action that pushes you beyond your own perceived boundaries of what is comfortable, familiar, and possible. The kind of action that supports your goals and at the same time makes you feel just a little uncomfortable as you're exploring your own new frontiers, whatever they may be. The kind of action that leads you to change your beliefs about who you are. . . and eventually allows you to conclude for yourself that who you are *right now* does not rely on what you do in any given area of life at any moment.

Who you are is your identity.

What you do is your role.

In the desert island exercise, no one asked about any role you could play or any relationship you could improve. All you were being asked about was your identity as a person—who you are. Not what you do!

So, now that you've considered this, did you give yourself a rating of less than 10?

When you started reading this chapter, did you start to make mental justifications to yourself about why you really did deserve less than a 10, as a person?

If so, it's definitely time to get to work. And the first and most essential piece of work is to separate your *role* from your *identity*.

In the realm of prospecting, in the realm of sales, or in any part of your life that now signals to you that your identity, as a person, is something less than a perfect 10 out of 10, you will now start to challenge yourself, make yourself just a little uncomfortable, and upgrade your beliefs about who you are—so that those beliefs are in line with reality. And the reality is that you are OK, just as you are.

As a person, you really are a 10 out of 10, whether you realize it or not. As a salesperson, or a cook, or an inventor, or a public speaker, or a marine biologist, or any other role you choose, you may well believe you rate less than a 10, and you may be right. Those are all roles. You may perform superbly within a given role, or you may see room for improvement in some area of that role. By the numbers, we may be a zero or we may be a 10 when we look at our role. But that number, wherever it falls, does not classify us when it comes to our identity as human beings. I'm repeating the point because it warrants repetition: As a person, I'm a 10. And so are you.

Here's a story that may help to illustrate the point.

## THE DANCE

Back in the old days, in school, we used to have these elaborate social rituals called *dances*. These dances were quite different from the closest modern equivalent, which would probably be concerts. In an era of strict separation of the sexes, dances, the kind we had, were really the major opportunity to meet and fraternize with members of the opposite sex. The two camps, male and female, would line up along opposite walls of the gymnasium, like opposing sports teams getting ready for a match.

Let's assume a guy named Bill is at one of those dances. Let's further assume that Bill's friends have been goading him all night to go up to a certain stunning blonde named Catherine and ask her to dance.

Bill's buddies started bugging him about this when the dance began, right around 8:00.

The dance ends at 11 P.M. What time do you think Bill is going to walk up to her and ask her to dance?

You've got it. 10:55 P.M.

At 10:55, Bill walks the 50 feet across the gym floor, and with every step he's convinced that all eyes are on him. In fact, to Bill, it doesn't feel like 50 feet at all.

It feels like 100 miles.

Bill makes it across. He asks Catherine to dance. She says, "No, thanks."

Now Bill has to walk back across that gym floor. The 50-foot walk feels like 200 miles this time. And with every step, what two words are pulsing through Bill's brain?

"Never again!"

That humiliating experience has convinced Bill that he is a loser.

Now let's say six months go by, and Bill's buddies invite him to another dance. Bill tells them he'll go but on one condition: "I never have to ask anybody to dance!"

So while he's there at the dance, Bill's friend Tom sidles up to Bill and says, "I bet you'd still like to dance with Catherine over there, right?"

Bill says, "Sure, but like I told you, I'm not about to cross that floor and ask her."

Tom says, "Hey, I've got an idea. Why don't I go ask her if she wants to dance with you?"

Bill tells him that sounds OK. Tom dutifully crosses the 50-foot gymnasium floor. As he does, how wide do you think the floor feels to him?

50 feet!

He asks Catherine whether she'll dance with Bill. She looks

across the gym floor to where Bill is standing, looks back at Tom, and gives Tom the same answer she gave Bill six months ago: "No, thanks."

Tom smiles and says, "Thanks anyway."

Undeterred, he goes over to the girl right beside Catherine, introduces himself, and asks for her name. It's Stephanie.

He says, "Hey, Stephanie, how about it? What would you think of a little charity work? Throw me a bone. Dance with my buddy Bill over there."

Stephanie looks across the gym floor, looks back at Tom, and says, "No, thanks." Tom smiles, thanks her, and moves on.

He repeats the procedure with Becky, Linda, and Juanita. He gets turned down every single time. After asking about a dozen girls on Bill's behalf, and striking out with every one of them, he walks back across the gym floor to the boys' side of the gym.

How wide does that floor feel to him as he walks back?

50 feet!

As he's walking, is he thinking "What a loser I am?"

No!

You know what he's thinking? "Hey. It ain't me. . . . I've just got a bad product to sell!"

## ROLE AND IDENTITY

Both of those efforts on the gym floor were "failures," but they were very different types of "failures."

Bill's was an identity failure. It was someone who failed as a person. Somewhere within that failure is a little six-year-old child who is angry and in pain.

Tom's was a role failure. Inside that one is an adult who has learned not to take the failure personally.

Prospecting effectively, selling effectively, is all about moving from a Bill mindset to a Tom mindset.

If you muddle together your identity and your role, it's very likely that you will stop taking (perceived) risks. You will feel like you failed as a person.

On the other hand, if you push your comfort zone enough to try some new things, build up some new insights and some new perspectives on yourself, and get a little more experience than you have now, you may eventually find that you've got an adult inside of you who will help you to grow, learn a little from each new experience, and not take setbacks personally.

## Changing Your Technique Is Not Enough!

The prospecting "technique" that I offer in this book has been proven successful in the field: thousands upon thousands of salespeople who "got" the Sandler principle managed to internalize those principles. You can learn the techniques, memorize them, even teach them to others. . . but until you've taken action, until you've *used* them to get beyond your existing zone of familiarity and comfort, until you've built up some new experiences and new benchmarks, until you've changed your attitudes and your beliefs to reflect the reality that, as a person, you are a 10 on a scale of 10, the techniques will be virtually useless!

At key points in this book, you'll be challenged to take specific action(s) to begin expanding your comfort/familiarity zone. Your ability to benefit from this book will depend completely on your own willingness to go for it, accept the challenge, take the action(s) described, and upgrade your own understanding of who you are and what you're capable of.

In the next chapter, you will
learn about "head trash."

# CHAPTER FOUR

## *Sandler Prospecting Principle #4: Clear out Your Head Trash*

Mark Twain once said, "It's not what we don't know that hurts us—it's what we know for sure that just ain't so." Whether he knew it or not, he was talking about head trash.

We all have head trash. People who sell for a living have head trash that is affecting their income. For them, clearing the trash out has to become both a personal and an economic priority!

It's very likely that you have two influential, pervasive pieces of head trash that relate directly to both selling and prospecting. Those two pieces of head trash took the form of the following limiting rules:

Rule number one: *Never talk to strangers.* Our mothers and fathers taught us that one when we were very young. It might have been appropriate to the situation back when we were children, but it's the kiss of death when it comes to making prospecting calls. In my case, I had to get rid of that head trash before I could improve my prospecting numbers. So do you.

Rule number two: *It is impolite to ask people about money—doing so will get you in trouble, get you slapped, or both.* I'm pretty sure my dad taught me this one when I asked him how much he paid for the champagne-gold 1969 Ford Falcon he bought used. I internalized this one really well, but I had to get rid of this head trash if I was going to prospect, or sell, with any effectiveness. So do you. The job description of the salesperson, when you get right down to it, is to ask people, "Do you have any money, and, if so, are you willing to give it to me?"

There are four steps to changing "head trash" beliefs. They are:

Step one: *Admit that you have head trash.* This is a little bit like attending an AA meeting. Say to yourself (or even better, right out loud to someone else) something like this: "Hi, my name is John Rosso, and I'm uncomfortable talking to strangers." You can skip the "Hi, my name is. . ." part, if you want, and you can even skip the part where you talk to somebody else, but you do have to find some way to explicitly acknowledge your own head trash. I have found that saying the words out loud really helps.

Step two: *Identify the head trash.* You've gotten a pretty good start on this one. Most of the salespeople I work with have some version of the two forms of head trash I just shared with you, and it's a pretty good bet that you do, too. It's also likely that there is other head trash waiting for you. (Another common example is, "I am not good at prospecting because I hate it." If that feels relevant, you can assume that you have successfully identified *three* pieces of head trash.)

Step three: *Decide that this is important enough to take action.* Either cleaning up the head trash matters enough for you to move on to step number four, below, or it doesn't. In my case, the numbers were abysmal enough that I wanted to do something to clean up the trash, so I committed to doing that. Whatever your personal "threshold" event is, you must reach it if you expect this or any other of the *action steps* in this book to deliver measurable improvements for you.

Step four: *Create and reinforce a new belief.* In step four, you build a new belief system you can get behind, you put it into words, and reinforce it every chance you get. For instance:

> "I have the (sales/operations/accounting/whatever) equivalent of a cure for cancer—other people have the right to know about it, and I have an obligation to tell them about it. Whatever they do with that information is up to them."

> "Money is the vocabulary of business. Business people are constantly talking about money, and they expect me to talk about money, too."

> "From this point forward, I only make calls that are warm to hot in nature." (This book is all about making warm calls.)

For me, these new beliefs replaced my old, self-created trashy rules. When I started the job of taking action and finding evidence for these two new rules, did I believe they were true? Of course not. But I wanted to believe they were true, accepted that they could be true, and the more evidence I found for them, the easier they became for me to adopt.

**In the next chapter, you will learn why discipline equals freedom.**

# CHAPTER FIVE

## Sandler Prospecting Principle #5: Discipline Equals Freedom

Getting rid of head trash is a lifelong task. You can start with the common unsupportive beliefs I've identified for you and then keep moving through your own personal head trash file. You'll probably never be finished. I guess it's just in the nature of human heads to generate trash.

The next principle, by contrast, is something you can check off the to-do list, each and every selling day. It's about setting your own personal activity targets for each working day.

You either hit those daily targets or you don't. If you do, you move closer to your financial goals. And I think you will agree that attaining your financial goals gives you more freedom in your life. At least when it comes to lifestyle and commission checks, discipline really does equal freedom.

The first, and most important, thing you can do before you begin any kind of prospecting routine is remove all the stress and guilt from the process. If you're feeling stressed and guilty, you're not going to have good discussions with prospective buyers. (I can tell you that from personal experience.)

If you have the discipline to set a measurable activity goal you want to accomplish today—say, having 10 new discussions with 10 new people you haven't talked to before—then you will have the freedom to embark on those 10 discussions—and then stop once you've hit them, without stress or guilt.

The magic of setting goals that connect to the right specific, measurable activity is that it relieves you of being responsible for the outcomes. You can't control what happens during those 10 discussions, but you can control whether or not you connect with 10 new people and talk to them! David Sandler used to challenge people to generate 25 "no" answers.

## THAT'S THE KIND OF GOAL I WANT YOU TO SET FOR YOURSELF TODAY.

Notice that I'm not asking you to generate one new *sale* today. That's an outcome. What I'm asking you to take responsibility for, and be disciplined about, is identifying a goal that connects to the activity that precedes the outcome and makes it possible.

Whatever goal you set, it should involve talking to new people on the telephone.

Even though I haven't shared any prospecting tactics with you yet, I still want you to set a (modest!) personal goal that connects to prospecting activity. It could be to talk to five new people, voice to voice, before the next working day is out. Whatever it is, I want you to commit the goal to writing, use your own personal discipline to follow through on it, and then experience the freedom that comes with knowing you have hit the mark, and are now free to do whatever else you want to do, guilt-free.

## Don't Make Excuses. Just Do It.

The daily creation of your own self-identified prospecting target, the acquisition of that target, and the ability to step away from the day guilt-free, knowing that you've done your best—these are the habits that turn around careers. And they're all about getting past the guilt.

When I was just getting started in sales, money was tight. After the bills were taken care of, I would set aside a specific amount—say, 100 bucks—that I could spend on anything I wanted, guilt-free. Two decades later, I realized that I was experiencing much more stress in my life, even though I had considerably more money to spend. Why? Because I wasn't being as disciplined in my spending habits. I wasn't identifying a specific amount that I could spend without guilt. I had lost control of my own process.

The same pattern plays out throughout the sales process. When we stop being disciplined, we experience stress and worry and lots of other negative emotions, and we start a self-perpetuating downward cycle.

Discipline really does equal freedom, in life and in selling. For us as salespeople, that discipline begins with setting our activity goals and our income goals. If we don't set the goal, we can't possibly know whether our actions are bringing us closer or taking us further away from it. (*NOTE:* A later principle, "just make the calls," depends on us knowing what our income target is and what steps we are going to take on a daily basis in order to go about achieving that goal.)

Create, and take action, on an activity-based prospecting

goal that you can measure. (For instance, you might set the goal of speaking to three new people you haven't spoken to before.) *Attain that goal today.*

Once you've done that, set your personal income goal for the next six months! Write it down!

> **In the next chapter, you will learn about the Buyer-Seller Dance.**

# CHAPTER SIX

## *Sandler Prospecting Principle #6: The Buyer-Seller Dance*

Most salespeople allow the prospect to lead the dance. In fact, what do most sales training systems tell us that the "selling process" should look like?

When I first learned about sales, I was told that the professional selling process was supposed to look like this:

| RAPPORT |
| --- |
| NEEDS |
| FEATURES AND BENEFITS PRESENTATION |
| RESOLVE OBJECTIONS/CLOSE |

That certainly seemed to make sense to me. As a salesperson, wasn't it my job to build rapport and then to uncover the prospect's needs? Wasn't I supposed to use what I had learned about those needs to build a presentation that highlighted the features and benefits that could satisfy those needs? Wasn't it then my job to close the sale and overcome any lingering objections?

The Sandler Selling System methodology taught me that there were some big problems with the traditional selling "system." I use quote marks because the "system" really isn't a system at all. It inevitably leads us to a situation where we are trying to close, but the prospect is, for some strange reason, coming up with brand-new objections, objections we never identified in the "needs" phase.

Suddenly there are objections about money, objections about timing, and objections about who can really make the decision. And then we find ourselves in the follow-up phase where we're trying to re-engage, regain momentum, and see if we can get a close, somehow, anyhow—perhaps by using some kind of psychological trick.

That's traditional selling: develop some rapport, uncover needs, present your features and benefits to fill those needs, attempt to gain commitment, handle all the objections. And then go back, follow up, and use a lot of closing tricks to attempt to regain commitment.

At times, it can become an endless loop.

Most of us will learn to sell this way, and on paper it looks OK.

In practice, there are some fundamental problems with it, though. The first and most important of these is that it mirrors the buyer's system.

The buyer's system is this: typically, while we're trying to generate interest, they tell us they're not interested and they put up a defense wall. That's step one.

If we get past that and into step two, they seem to be talking about their "needs," but what is really happening is that they are picking our brains for information, which amounts to what we call "unpaid consulting."

As we prepare our dog and pony show for our so-called value-added solution (stage three), they get a wonderful education. Mind you, they don't pay for it. Nor do they make any commitments about what they're going to do with that education once they get it.

Then we move to step four, where we try to simultaneously close and deal with any outstanding objections that may come up. Very often, during this step, we encounter a brand-new objection that seems to come out of left field. Or maybe people sound as if they're giving us a commitment, but it tends to be a meaningless no-commitment. What the prospect says may use positive words, but the commitment actually has no teeth.

The buyer's no-commitment commitment might sound like this: "All things being equal, apples to apples, Lord willing and the creek don't rise, I don't see any reason why we wouldn't go forward and do this. . . but I need to think about it. Give me a couple weeks or so, and then let's follow up in, uh, the second week of March."

And then we make that last call to follow up, and all of the sudden we find that our prospect has entered the Witness Protection Program. We leave a voice mail message, and we get no voice mail message back. We follow up again, and we get a list of excuses. The decision maker is out to lunch, in a meeting, in the restroom, in Kuala Lampur, on vacation. It's like there's a list of 17 things to say when Joe Salesperson calls: "Let's see. This is the fifth call, so tell him Joe's out of the office."

We get stuck in this Buyer-Seller Dance. And guess what? The buyer is leading the dance.

Before you move on, identify one recent sequence of discussions you engaged in where the prospect was leading the "sales" process. It shouldn't be hard to come up with. Write down what happened before you move on.

> **In the next chapter, you will learn about two different kinds of rapport.**

# CHAPTER SEVEN

## *Sandler Prospecting Principle #7: Fake Rapport vs. Real Rapport*

What if there was a selling system that matched up, not with the prospect's buying process, but with what you as a professional salesperson were actually trying to accomplish at any given moment?

What if there was a selling system that, if you followed it, made it literally impossible to get stuck in the Buyer-Seller Dance?

There is. And we'll begin exploring it right now. You will find that, when it is implemented faithfully, this system is incredibly effective. But there's a catch: to take advantage of it, you've got to be willing to break some of the selling "rules" you may have learned in the past. The first, and perhaps the most important of the rules you will have to be willing to break, has to do with the much-abused topic of *rapport.*

Now, please don't misunderstand. As salespeople, we do have

to create rapport with our prospects, our customers, and any number of other people in our lives. But we have to create *real* rapport. Unfortunately, what we've been trained to do by the selling "rules" that have been drummed into us over time by various self-appointed sales experts, and perhaps by our own prospects and customers, is to create *fake* rapport.

At this point, you're probably wondering what the difference between real rapport and fake rapport is. The answer is actually quite simple: Real rapport creates an environment that is comfortable enough for two parties to take part in a discussion as functional equals. Fake rapport doesn't do that.

Fake rapport during the early phase of a prospecting call might sound like this: "I took a look at your Web site, and may I just say, I was very, very impressed, Mr. Prospect."

This kind of remark, when placed at the beginning of a conversation with someone who is—let's face it—still a total stranger, fails the real-rapport standard.

It fails in at least two ways. First, it doesn't make the prospect feel comfortable enough to hold a real business discussion with us as a functional equal because it is transparently inauthentic. Most qualified decision makers will see right through the flattery. They'll think, "Yeah, right. I bet you say that to all the girls." Usually, they'll be right.

The second way that this kind of statement fails us is that it doesn't really make us feel like the other person's functional equal. It can't possibly establish us as someone who really has a right to hold a one-on-one discussion with the decision maker. Why not? Because it's begging for validation. We are seeking OK-ness.

Fake rapport during prospecting calls is the telephone equivalent of walking into the prospect's office, looking at the family photos on the person's desk, pasting a plastic smile on our face, and saying, "Gosh, what beautiful kids." What we say may be accurate or it may not be, but since it isn't heartfelt, it does not create a bond between equals. In reality, the fact that we're choosing to say something like this it at the beginning of a business relationship makes us stink of fear and thus puts us in a subservient position, which is the exact opposite of where we want to be.

As a result, this kind of remark falls into the category of fake rapport. It's not real. It's not authentic to who we are or why we're calling. Instead, it's a plea for acceptance. It's actually an apology for making the call in the first place, disguised as a compliment—a compliment that the other person undoubtedly realizes is completely insincere.

Establishing real rapport, rapport between functional equals who are willing to consider themselves and each other OK, is a very different skill.

Mastering this skill is not a footnote to the sales process, not a matter of memorizing and reciting a single catchphrase. In fact, mastering real rapport is what makes the entire sales process possible.

Here's an interesting exercise. Identify at least three sales appeals you received that used "rapport-building" strategies that actually created *fake* rapport. What actually happened in those exchanges? Did you buy from him or not? Write the answers in the spaces below.

1. _____
2. _____
3. _____

We face a big challenge. During any prospecting phone call, we have to find ways to create real rapport. Not fake rapport! Real rapport, as we have seen, is the kind of rapport based on developing an environment of trust, comfort, credibility, and peer-to-peer status with the person we're calling. How do we do that?

By being authentic.

Believe it or not, being authentic takes some practice. A whole lot of salespeople probably think that they're being authentic by saying things like, "May I just say, I was very, very impressed by your Web site today." A clue that this isn't authentic comes when the prospect says to them, "Gee, that's odd, because our Web site has been down for maintenance for the last few days."

You might also think you're being authentic when you ask a question like this: "How are you today?" If you aren't willing to listen for 20 minutes as the other person tells you, in detail, exactly how the day has gone, then you might want to think of another question. This one is so overused that, even if you really do mean it, it automatically smells inauthentic.

One of the best ways to be authentic is to learn to be disarmingly honest. That means learning to say things that are true but do not appear to be in your best interests to say.

People are sometimes a little skeptical when we suggest that they say things that seem to go against their own interests during a sales call. Here's a little exercise that will illustrate exactly what this means and how this (powerful) principle works.

For the purposes of this exercise, I want you to pretend that I'm your prospect and that I currently work with your chief competitor. We'll call that competitor X.

And I say, "I am currently working with competitor X, and I'm relatively happy with what X is doing for me. At the same time, I'm open-minded to new alternatives. I don't know much about your organization, but I'm willing to learn." So, during your initial call to me, the prospect, I ask you a pointed question: "What are the top two or three reasons why I should be working with you?"

We've done this exercise with countless salespeople, and when we have asked this question during live programs, we tend to hear the exact same answers, regardless of the industry or the level of experience of the salespeople with which we're working. Here's what they say:

- Quality
- Service
- One-stop shop
- Reputation
- Expertise
- Financial stability
- Legacy/industry connections
- Resources/support
- Competitive pricing

Did any of those words come to mind as *your* answer to the question, "What are the two or three best reasons for me to consider working with you?"

I thought so.

Now, as we continue this scenario, I've got some good news and some bad news for you. Here's the bad news: You're fired! Your company was downsizing, and they decided to let you go.

And here's the good news: a few days later, you were hired by your most worthy competitor, X.

So now let's do the same thing all over again. Now, I'm a different prospect, but I ask you the same question. . . only this time, I'm asking you about X. I say, "Tell me: what are the top two or three reasons why I should be working with X?"

As a salesperson working for X, your former competitor, what would you say?

Surprise, surprise. History has shown you're going to respond with something from this list:

- Quality
- Service
- One-stop shop
- Reputation
- Expertise
- Financial stability
- Legacy/industry connections
- Resources/support
- Competitive pricing

Looks familiar, doesn't it?

Do you see a problem here? The prospect has heard all of this before and knows he will hear it again the very next time a salesperson from another company calls!

On a scale of credibility where zero is the prospect saying out loud, "Liar, everybody says that," and 10 is angels singing above the prospect's head while the prospect says, "Wow! You've got that? You have quality? Where do I sign?" where would you rank the credibility you inspire when you say something from this list?

Most people give us the numbers three, four, or five. Some even say one or two. In other words, low or mediocre credibility, which means fake rapport.

Face it: There is a huge credibility gap between you and the prospective buyer, one that opens the minute the other person realizes you're selling something. Most salespeople ignore that gap and pretend it isn't there. You're not going to do that, though.

Let's look again at how this credibility gap opens. Even if your competitor doesn't have, say, the highest quality, what do you think *they're* saying in response to the question, "Why should I work with you?"

Do you think they're saying: "Well, it's certainly not the quality because our stuff is junk. It's not our financial viability, either, because we can go out of business any minute"?

No!

Even if those things happened to be true, salespeople working for your competition couldn't say that. In fact, many of them will say or imply the exact opposite, which is why most of the people you want to talk to have decided, even before you pick up the phone to call, that they simply can't trust salespeople.

Prospective buyers view this whole process as dysfunctional. And you know what? We can't blame them. They have lots of evidence for that belief. To give them evidence in the other direction, we have to break the rules. . . and be disarmingly honest. That means being honest enough to create real peer-to-peer rapport.

Here's an example of how this might sound during the initial phase of a prospecting call:

Person you called: Bill, I currently work with competitor X, but I'm open to alternatives. I don't know much about your company. Why should I work with you?

Now imagine saying something like this in response:

Salesperson: Greg, I appreciate you asking me that question, and I could give you a lot of reasons why we have generated a loyal customer base over the years. They tell us they appreciate our service after the sale. They appreciate our diverse line of products, and the ability to get everything in one stop. But realistically. . .

. . . depending upon what you're getting today from your supplier, and some of the things that you're looking for, I don't know the answer to that. You might be best served staying where you are.

Can I make a suggestion? Can we back up just a couple of steps? Let me ask you some fairly straightforward questions about what you're looking for in the area of widgets, and give you a chance to pick my brain, so we could figure out whether we truly could add real value by working with you. And if the answer is *no*, that's OK... *because we're not for everyone.*

And Greg, if the answer's *yes*, then you and I could spend the last couple of minutes together on this call thinking about what would be the best way to start a business relationship and begin. Are you OK with all that?

Was what you just read more credible or less credible than responding with, "People buy from us because we offer one-stop shopping"?

Was what you just read more likely to produce real rapport, or less likely?

If you're like most of the salespeople we train, you will agree that what I have just shown you is a much better way to build rapport than what you're currently using; because this method increases your credibility, it lowers the buyer's defense wall, and it starts a dialogue.

Those are both good outcomes, but remember that memorizing and reciting my words, rather than yours, will likely make you sound less authentic, not more authentic. You'll be getting more insights on how to use what you've just learned in later principles.

> ### In the next chapter, you will learn more about Bonding and Rapport.

# CHAPTER EIGHT

## Sandler Prospecting Principle #8: Two Pieces of the Puzzle

 little earlier in this book, I asked you to "unlearn" this familiar sales model:

| RAPPORT |
| --- |
| NEEDS |
| FEATURES AND BENEFITS PRESENTATION |
| RESOLVE OBJECTIONS/CLOSE |

Trying to follow this sales model virtually guarantees that you will end up wasting precious time in the *Buyer-Seller Dance* we discussed.

There is another huge reason to reject this model, however, and

I hope it is obvious to you now. Notice that the first step, which goes by any number of names in any number of different systems, is all about rapport. The implication is that, once you get rapport out of the way, you can then move on to gathering information, presenting your proposal, and closing the deal.

This is false. Even assuming that you create real peer-based rapport in the early moments of (for instance) a prospecting call, you can lose that rapport just as quickly. The reality is that you must constantly re-establish peer-based rapport throughout your sales process. If you lose it, the sales cycle stops cold.

Don't think of rapport building as a separate step you can "complete" but as a kind of fuel that allows you to make forward progress in the sale. It's not a location on the sales process roadmap; it's something that makes it possible for you to reach your destination with the prospect.

Peer-based rapport is a "missing piece of the puzzle." No wonder so many salespeople have trouble establishing real rapport! They think of it as something you check off the list. It's not. It's a tank you need to refill constantly.

This is one piece of the puzzle that often gets overlooked.

There's another piece of the puzzle that's missing in that traditional model, however, and it's almost as important as rapport. This second "missing piece of the puzzle" is another kind of fuel that moves your sales process forward. It works in concert with peer-based rapport. It can be found in the role-play response that I shared with you in the previous chapter.

In the response that follows, you'll notice that two of the phrases in italic accomplish the "disarming honesty" goal I shared with you in the previous chapter. One of those phrases, however, does a very different kind of job.

Look at it again.

Salesperson: Greg, I appreciate you asking me that question, and I could give you a lot of reasons why we have generated a loyal customer base over the years. They tell us they appreciate (yada yada yada). Depending upon what you're getting today from your supplier, and some of the things that you're looking for, I don't know the answer to that. *(1) You might be best served staying where you are.*

Can I make a suggestion? Can we back up just a couple of steps? Let me ask you some fairly straightforward questions about what you're looking for in the area of widgets, and give you a chance to pick my brain, so we could figure out whether we could add real value by working with you. *(2) And if the answer is no, that's OK… because we're not for everyone.*

And Greg, if the answer's *yes*, then you and I could spend the last couple of minutes together on this call thinking about what would be the best way to start a business relationship and begin. *(3) Are you OK with all that?*

In the response you just read, one of the three numbered phrases is not an example of "disarming honesty." Was it number one, number two, or number three?

**In the next chapter, you will learn all about the Up-Front Contract.**

# CHAPTER NINE

## *Sandler Prospecting Principle #9: The Up-Front Contract*

Of course, I do not want you to memorize my words, but I do want you to *notice* what's going on in that example you just read. Check it out again: **"You might be best served staying where you are."**

What's happening here? Well, that's disarming honesty. Why? Because most sales calls don't acknowledge that the competition may well be the best fit for the prospect! This is not the kind of thing a salesperson typically says to a prospect. It's the kind of thing a peer says to a peer.

By the way, notice that I'm not talking about using *brutal* honesty. That would sound like this: "Greg, we're four times as expensive as our nearest competitor, and our quality is only half what theirs is." Save those kinds of facts for a conversation with your company's senior leadership about how you can improve your product and/or service offerings!

Let's go back again to the response.

## "We're Not for Everyone."

This, again, is disarming honesty. Not all salespeople volunteer the fact that they are not for everyone. It's the kind of talk you expect from a functional equal—not from someone who's out to "close the deal" at any cost, every possible time. That would be a childish impulse; this, on the other hand, is an adult talking to an adult.

Notice what has also emerged at this point: As an adult, we're beginning to sketch out a plan for what could come next. Watch what we do with that plan.

**"And Greg, if the answer's *yes*, then you and I could spend the last couple of minutes together on this call thinking about what would be the best way to start a business relationship and begin. Are you OK with all that?"**

With the phrase "Are you OK with all that?"—or any of the countless personalized variations you may come up with—we come upon the second form of fuel for forward motion in the sales process: the up-front contract.

This is the heart of the Sandler System. It's an agreement, in advance, about what's going to happen next. Depending on where you are in the sales cycle, what happens next could be big (you get a signed contract), or it could be comparatively small (the other person agrees to answer your questions and discuss the possibility of a business relationship).

**An up-front contract is an agreement in advance about what will take place when you and the prospect interact.** When you propose an up-front contract, you are clarifying the expectations for both participants in the exchange. . . and confirming your status as the functional equal of the person to whom you're talking.

The up-front contract is all about clarifying "what happens next" so that there is no room for doubt. In the case of a prospecting discussion, which is the focus of this book, *what happens next* is generally an agreement to keep talking and exploring and then make a decision.

Like bonding and rapport, up-front contracts are not a single step you check off the list and then forget about. **Up-front contracts must be an integral and continuous part of your prospecting process and your sales process.**

Up-front contracts must make the following things perfectly clear:

- What you're expecting to take place and what the prospect is expecting to take place.
- How much time you have.
- What the agenda should be as you talk.
- What decisions will be made at the end of your conversation.

. We'll be exploring the specifics of the up-front contract in much more detail later on in the book. For now, just remember that this agreement is the second essential form of "fuel" for your sales process. In a way, bonding and rapport and up-front contracts are really two sides of the same coin. Bonding and rapport means developing an environment of trust, comfort, credibility and functional equality with the prospect; setting an up-front contract means acting on, and reinforcing, that environment of emotional comfort between peers. How? By proposing what you think should happen next and then listening to what the other person has to say about what you've proposed.

The key word there is *listening;* it ties together both of these ideas. We'll explore how listening supports both bonding and rapport and the up-front contract in the next chapter.

- Using your own words, create written bullet points that enable you to answer the prospect's question: "Why should

I buy from you when I'm satisfied with my present supplier?"

- Make sure your response (1) establishes bonding and rapport and (2) proposes an up-front contract.
- Practice answering the question out loud, in your own
  words.

**In the next chapter, you will learn
about the Sandler Submarine.**

# CHAPTER TEN

## *Sandler Prospecting Principle #10: The Sandler Submarine*

W hat do we know by now about the ideal sales process? We know that one kind of "fuel" for that process is the act of establishing bonding and rapport. This is the answer to the question: "How do I develop an environment of trust, comfort, credibility, and equal business stature on an on-going basis?"

We know, too, that the second kind of fuel is the up-front contract. As we saw in the previous chapter, this is merely an agreement in advance, between peers, about what both sides can expect to happen during a given interaction. Like the bonding and rapport piece, with which it overlaps, the up-front contract needs to take place throughout the sales process. In fact, these two closely related processes are what propel the sales process forward.

And we also know that listening is essential to anyone who

hopes to create bonding and rapport or gain agreement on an up-front contract. Without active listening, you are out of fuel, and your sales process sputters to a halt! Most people think they have better listening skills than they actually do. This is notably true among salespeople.

> *"The single biggest problem in communication is the illusion that it has taken place."*
> **–George Bernard Shaw**

One important point about bonding and rapport and the up-front contract bears endless repeating, so please forgive me as I emphasize it again: these are not "steps" of a process that you can do once and check off your to-do list. When they stop, the sales process itself stops!

David Sandler put these two critical elements first in his famous Sandler Submarine, which is a visual representation of the Sandler Selling System model.

The reason Sandler used a submarine as a metaphor for selling was that he loved the old World War II action movies where the submarine came under attack from enemy torpedoes. Maybe you've seen one of those movies. The classic scene looks like this: Alerted to a breach in one part of the submarine, the men mobilize, fight through the rushing water, move into a watertight compartment, and seal off the special door with great effort. The breach has been contained. The submarine can keep on moving ahead!

That kind of containment, that "watertightness," is what a good sales system should be doing for us. It should allow us to totally seal off each compartment as we make our way through the discussion with the prospect and keep moving forward. This is the ideal sales process: one that doesn't stall or go backwards, one that doesn't (for instance) deliver brand-new objections when you thought you were in the "closing stage."

Take a look at the Sandler Submarine now, and notice what comes right after the two "fuel cells" we've already identified.

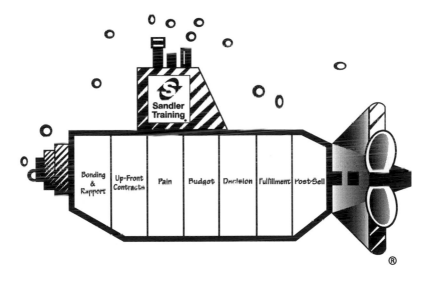

What "compartment" is positioned right after Bonding and Rapport and Up-Front Contracts in the Sandler Submarine?

**In the next chapter, you will learn about that compartment.**

# CHAPTER ELEVEN

## Sandler Prospecting Principle #11: The Pain Step

It's time for a reality check. We need to be clear on something: I am assuming that, for the purposes of this book, your job is *not* to close the sale over the phone. (That would be *Telesales the Sandler Way*.) Our goal here is to *prospect*, which means, when you get right down to it, that our goal is to create enough rapport to build a scheduled up-front contract to meet or talk again at a certain point in time.

That makes sense, doesn't it? Yet, to schedule that discussion, we have to understand the whole sales process we will eventually be leading the prospect through. . . and that means understanding each compartment of the Sandler Submarine.

At the end of the last chapter, I asked you to identify the compartment right next to Up-Front Contracts on that submarine. It is, of course, Pain.

A lot of people misunderstand this step. They imagine it's concerned with identifying the discomfort or inconvenience experienced when a given product, service, or solution is not working at peak efficiency. Or isn't working at all. Or hasn't been implemented in the first place. For instance, the bus you ride to get to work each morning consistently arrives late. You put up with it. You become accustomed to it. You build the bus being late into your day. That's not pain, at least not the kind of pain David Sandler was talking about. He was talking about the *emotional* gap between where you are and where you want to be.

Sandler's great breakthrough—and the quote for which he is most famous—is that "people make buying decisions emotionally and then justify those decisions intellectually." This is a basic fact of human behavior, and it has implications that extend far beyond the selling realm. It is true of every major (and minor) life decision I've ever made, and I strongly suspect the same can be said for everyone reading this book. Emotions propel our decisions; logic confirms them. Interestingly, we now know from science that people whose emotional systems have been severely compromised by brain injury literally cannot make decisions, even about trivial issues.

For our purposes, though, you and I are interested in the forces that trigger emotional purchasing decisions that people will eventually justify intellectually. Now, if you look back on the sales you yourself have closed over the course of your career, and examine each one carefully, you will find that, in most or maybe even all of the cases, the person who made the decision to buy from you did so to avoid some present or future experience of pain. At least eight times out of ten, in my experience, that's what drove the emotion—and the decision. (The remaining two times out of 10, I'm willing to bet, the person bought from you to preserve some pleasurable experience, or to ensure that a pleasurable experience took place at some point in the future. (That's an emotionally-driven decision, too, of course.)

The Pain Step is the discovery process where we identify the emotional triggers that are relevant to this particular buyer and show us what pain he is willing to take action to avoid. The Pain Step is, by its very nature, a highly personalized process where we identify the compelling emotional reasons that motivate an individual buyer to take action to close the gap between where he is now and where he wants to be.

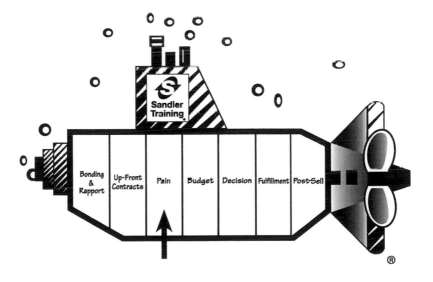

Pain is what you are out to identify on this call. As a practical matter, *most* of your successful prospecting calls will help you to establish some rapport, set up an initial up-front contract, identify an initial pain or two, and then, based on that, set up a second up-front contract that connects to a later, scheduled meeting or discussion to which you can both commit.

But you really need to understand the whole submarine before you can make that call! Otherwise you won't know where you are or where you're going when you get into a discussion with this person.

What pains do you solve in your business? (Identify at least three, in writing.)

What "compartment" is positioned right after Pain in the Sandler Submarine?

**In the next chapter, you will learn
about that compartment.**

# CHAPTER TWELVE

## *Sandler Prospecting Principle #12: The Budget Step*

The objective of the next "compartment," the Budget Step, is to uncover whether the buyer is both willing and able to make any and all investments necessary to move forward in the relationship. This is where a lot of salespeople go astray. They invest a lot of time and energy in relationships where either the willingness or the ability to invest in their solution is lacking.

Of course, it's possible for someone to be willing, but unable, to move forward. That situation sounds like this: "You know, we actually want to do it, but we don't have the money."

It's also possible to be able but unwilling: "We have the money, but we don't want to spend it with you."

The Budget compartment is where we work together with the other person, as a peer, to confirm that (a) there's an opportunity that's compelling enough for each of us to want to take action on and invest our various resources in, and that (b) *both of us* are in fact capable of taking action. This conversation usually takes a little time and trust. It's unlikely to play out completely during an initial phone call.

The Budget Step is where we begin to ask questions like: what are the constraints to moving forward?

The answer to this question is not always about money. There are lots of other investments to consider. Are they willing and able to invest time? Attention? Political capital? Access to stakeholders? Last but not least, what are *we* willing to invest? This compartment is where we propose some broad ranges to give the decision maker a chance to understand what all those investments are likely to look like, so we can both start looking frankly at whether or not those investments are realistic. Very often, when it comes to evaluating whether specific financial investments are realistic, it makes sense to use a technique called "bracketing." You can make an estimate that the investment will be between X and Y, based on what you now know, and narrow the range as you get more and more information and build up more and more mutual trust.

Let me repeat: unless you are aiming to close sales over the phone—and again, that's not really what this book is about,—it's unlikely that you will complete this budget stage of the submarine during your phone calls.

It's not *impossible* that you'll get here during a prospecting call. We work with lots of salespeople who start out with the aim of setting the appointment and end up closing the deal over the phone! These days, when so much "selling" takes place over long distances, or via video calls, that's an outcome worth being open to. So it really does make sense to understand the whole Sandler Submarine. You must always know where you are and what compartment you've just sealed off!

Prospecting the Sandler way requires that you know *why* you're setting an up-front contract at the beginning of the call, *why* you're setting another up-front contract at the end of the call, and *what* comes next. With that in mind, let's take a closer look at the rest of the Sandler Submarine.

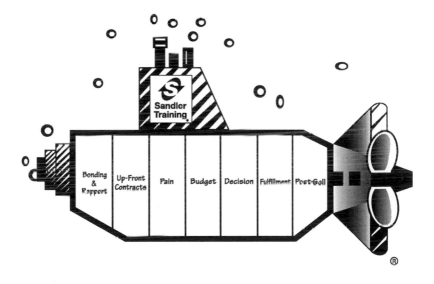

Take another look at the Sandler Submarine. What "compartment" is positioned right after Budget?

**In the next chapter, you will learn about that compartment.**

# CHAPTER THIRTEEN

## *Sandler Prospecting Principle #13: The Decision Step*

In the previous chapter, your job was to find the next "compartment" in the Sandler Submarine, the one that comes right after the Budget Step. If you're reading these words, I'm hoping that's because you found it: Decision.

Here's a painful but necessary truth: the vast majority of salespeople can find the word "decision" in the submarine graphic, but they don't find out anything meaningful about the prospect's decision-making process in the real world.

Here's what usually happens: after a cursory initial discussion that usually skips the Pain and Budget Steps altogether, they rush into the so-called "proposal stage" without bothering to find out what will happen as a result of their delivering that proposal.

They have no idea whether what they're putting into the proposal is what the prospect actually needs to see, hear, and experience *in order to make a good decision.* They have no idea who will actually be deciding what happens next. Usually, they deliver their "proposal" to someone who has no authority whatsoever to implement it! Then they wonder why nothing happens.

That, as I say, is how most salespeople work. They rush to the proposal. We definitely don't want to be one of those salespeople! We have to understand what needs to happen in this critical Decision Step. Otherwise, we will very likely be following the prospect's sales process and not our own sales process.

Completing the Decision Step is a matter of getting a complete and accurate understanding of the process that will lead us to either a *yes* or a *no* answer.

Important: We are interested not just in a prospect's decision to write out a check and do business with us. We also want to understand the whole chain of little decisions that connect to that big decision.

That's why, early on in the development cycle, we must discover the who, what, when, where, how, and why of the prospect's complete buying process. Again, most of the time, you won't have to focus on any of this during your prospecting call. But you do need to focus on it after you complete the Budget Step.

To whom are we talking? What are the steps of their process? What are the associated time lines? Where in the organizational chart will the final decision be made? Who would be involved in this process? Are we talking to the right people? If not, how do we expand our network of influence? How have they made decisions like this in the past? What criteria are they using to make this decision now? Why those criteria? What specifically is going to happen next? How do we know?

If we don't know the answers to those questions, we're really in no position to make a recommendation. We are investing significant time, effort, energy, and expertise in this process. We have a right—and a duty—to get clear answers to these questions. We do so in the Decision Step.

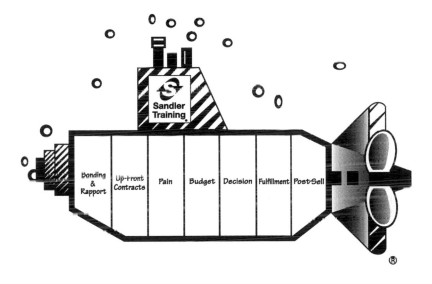

You're on a roll! What compartment is positioned right after Decision in the Sandler Submarine?

In the next chapter, you will learn about that compartment.

# CHAPTER FOURTEEN

## Sandler Prospecting Principle #14: The Fulfillment Step

Most salespeople (and most selling systems) really get lost in the woods at this stage. They get distracted by that dog and pony show they call a "presentation." They figure that, just because they've delivered this "presentation," they must have crossed some kind of major psychological threshold with the prospective buyer. So they deliver the magic words. . . . Then they wonder why this supposedly new stage of the selling process feels a whole lot like a brushoff.

We shake hands. People say nice things to each other. Then, most of the time, nothing happens. There may be talk. But there is no action.

After you (supposedly) complete your "presentation" stage, have you ever heard your prospect backing away from a decision? It might sound like this: "Hmm. You know what? This was very interesting. You've given me a whole lot to think about. Let me sleep on this/talk to my board of directors about this/talk to my spouse about this/ talk to my analyst about this/spend a month or so on a mountain-top communing with the Almighty about this. . . and I'll be back in touch with you soon to let you know where we come down on it."

Not really, though.

As I hope you will clearly see by now, that "prospect" is, in all likelihood, about to pull a disappearing act.

And do you know why?

Because you completely misunderstood what your goal was in this part of the sale. David Sandler believed that a huge part of that misunderstanding is rooted in the bad name most salespeople have given to this part of the process: presentation.

Maybe we thought our big goal was simply to deliver a presenta-tion. But actually our goal when we reach this point of the sale is two-fold. Assuming we have done our work up front and either qualified or disqualified the opportunity (by identifying both the resources and the decision-making process), we now have these two jobs:

1. Establishing an up-front contract to get either a clear "yes" decision or a clear "no" decision about whether or not to do business together.
2. Presenting a solution that truly takes care of the pain we've identified.

These two jobs are interconnected. Once we deliver our view of what that solution looks like, we get an unambiguous answer based on our up-front contract. That's the deal.

David Sandler's challenge to you, me, and every salesperson on Earth is to stop thinking of this part of the sale as the place where we present our proposal (and—did you notice?—take all the risks and do all the work) and start thinking about it as the place where fulfillment of mutual needs and expectations begins to take place.

If we get a *no*, that's OK. We're grownups. We realize that what we offer is not going to be for everyone. At least we know where we stand.

If we get a *yes*, that's certainly OK, too.

Fulfillment is where both seller and prospect start moving forward, based on peer-to-peer agreements. A lot of people refer to this mutual commitment as the "closing" phase.

By the way, if you thought the "selling process" stopped at the moment you got a clear commitment to buy, there's a surprise in store for you.

We're nearly done with the Sandler Submarine. What compartment is positioned right after Fulfillment?

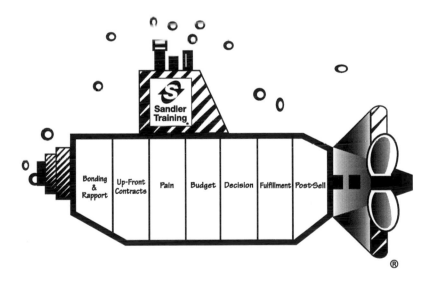

In the next chapter, you will learn
about that compartment.

# CHAPTER FIFTEEN

## *Sandler Prospecting Principle #15: The Post-Sell Step*

You may not have expected to find a step after the point in the sale where you heard the word "yes," but you just did. It's called the Post-Sell, and you're going to need to understand it if you expect to prospect (or sell) the Sandler way. Why? Because, before you sell anything else, you are selling an appointment!

As salespeople, we are often explicitly trained to "get the *yes* and get out." In other words, once we receive a commitment from a prospect, our job is to get the handshake, the signature, and the delivery (or startup date) just as quickly as we can, and then (let's be honest) vanish before anything bad happens.

Does that really sound like the kind of relationship you want to launch here?

David Sandler took a very different approach. He trained us

to believe that if we get a *yes*, we have to "post-sell" that decision. We have to give the prospect a series of verbal rehearsal steps to make sure that they don't back out. We have to do something that most salespeople avoid doing, which is: ask, after we've come to an agreement, whether the prospect can think of any reason he might decide to walk away from that agreement.

Read that again, because it's really what you have to do. Shortly after that critical moment when you do secure an agreement to buy, you have to ask the prospect, right out loud, if he can think of any reason—any reason at all—that the deal would fall through. And then you have to stop talking and listen to what the other person says.

So for instance, if I'm displacing a competitor, I have to find out from my prospect exactly what it would take for that prospect to decide to go back to that competitor. Believe it or not, my willingness to ask that question and initiate that conversation, which most salespeople avoid, actually makes it *easier* for the prospect to do all the things he is going to have to do to finalize the move away from my competitor.

If you think about it, you will realize that this post-sell discussion really is an essential step. Why? Because, whether you like it or not, the prospect *is* going to review all the possible reasons for walking away from the deal you've just made shortly after he or she shakes hands with you. The only question is whether he is going to do that alone, or during a conversation with you! I'd much rather be part of that conversation than not be part of it. If you stop to consider the matter closely, you'll realize that you want to be part of that conversation, too.

The truth is nothing has "closed" at all when you hear the first *yes*. A mutually profitable relationship has begun. In the Post-Sell Step, you set the ground rules for that mutually profitable, ongoing relationship.

As you will see shortly, this principle carries through to the prospecting phone call. It is *not* limited to the moment when you get a formal commitment to purchase your product or service.

Name all the compartments of the Sandler Submarine, in order, without looking at the pictures in the earlier chapters. If you find you can't do it, practice until you can!

**In the next chapter, you will internalize and "lock down" what you've learned so far.**

# CHAPTER SIXTEEN

## *Sandler Prospecting Principle #16: The Compass*

I hope you now know the various compartments of the submarine. With any luck, and with some practice over time, it should become second nature. That takes practice. And practice is what this principle is all about.

Practice is the key to mastering the stress-free prospecting call. Practice is the *only* way you will be able to internalize what you've learned thus far. And you *must* internalize—not just know about but *live in*—the Sandler Submarine if you hope to implement what I'll be sharing with you in future principles.

Once again, I want you to name all the compartments of the Sandler Submarine, in order, without looking at the picture. If you can do that, read on!

When you understand the components of the Sandler Submarine at an instinctive level, you can begin to assess where you really are and what you are really doing with a prospect. You can use the submarine model as a directional tool, as a kind of sales compass.

With a little practice, you will find that this compass-equipped submarine will not only tell you whether you are going where you are supposed to be going but also whether you are doing what you are supposed to be doing.

The more often you use the compass that's built into this, the better you will get at reading it and using it. The key point here is practice. David Sandler once said, "You can't teach a kid to ride a bicycle at a seminar." He meant that knowing about the Sandler Submarine is not the same as experiencing it. We must take action and implement it in a personal sense.

Our entire sales discussion with the prospect must be driven by this model. We must create rapport and bond with the prospect; we must propose and win up-front contracts throughout the sale. Those two elements must fuel the entire conversation.

We must identify pain. We must talk about the budget, which means talking about all the various kinds of investment both sides will be making in order to work together. We must identify the real decision-making process. We must pass the fulfillment test. And we must post-sell in a way that begins a long-term relationship, rather than simply closing a sale.

That's the sale as a whole. Now, what about the prospecting discussion?

**In the next chapter, you will learn about the structure of your prospecting call.**

# CHAPTER SEVENTEEN

## *Sandler Prospecting Principle #17: The Mini-Submarine*

The prospecting discussion, which typically (but not always) takes place on the phone, can be thought of as a "mini-submarine." It's also equipped with a compass. And it's designed to go in exactly the same direction. North is still north. But the mini-submarine's job is just to get us to the face-to-face meeting or scheduled first discussion.

On a prospecting call, we're driving a mini-sub. We will use *parts* of the big submarine.

During this call, we will establish rapport and create a bond; we will create and win an up-front contract about the call itself; we will uncover some of the prospect's pain; we will ask the prospect directly to make an investment in the form of more time, so we can get together. We will set another up-front contract for the next discussion. And we will post-sell that up-front contract so that the prospect doesn't cancel the appointment.

Then, you will implement the Sandler Selling System methodology without skipping any steps at all. But the vehicle that can *get* you there (while you're still on the phone, at any rate) is that miniature submarine.

Once you understand how the big submarine works, you can learn how to navigate the miniature submarine.

Before we start that navigation lesson, though, it's time for an important assignment.

Post the big submarine graphic in your working area, where you can see it every day. Place an X next to the Bonding and Rapport, Up-Front Contract, Pain, and Post-Sell compartments.

Then create a list of 20 prospects you want to call but have not yet called. Place each person's name and contact information at the top of a single piece of paper. Then hit the computer and devote an hour to learning as much as you possibly can about each of those prospects by using online search and networking tools such as Google, LinkedIn, YouTube and Twitter. Limit your research to professionally-relevant information.

Internet homework for each of your 20 designated prospects could include:

- What online articles, publications, or presentations has this person created?
- To what professional organizations does this person belong? (Pay particularly close attention to memberships in relevant organizations, such as a local chamber of commerce.)
- Does this person know anyone who is in your professional network?
- To what professionally-relevant discussion groups does the person lead or contribute?

- What is this person's career history... recent and long-term? (Pay particularly close attention to recent promotions.)
- What else can you discover about the company for which this person works?

(For more help with pre-call research online, see Appendix A: Three Tips for Effective Online Searches.)

**In the next chapter, you will learn about the strategic goals of your prospecting call.**

# CHAPTER EIGHTEEN

## *Sandler Prospecting Principle #18: The Contact Development Plan*

S
o let's get one thing straight. I am not going to ask you to do any "cold calling,"—ever. Instead, what I am going to ask you to do is to create a workable phone strategy for *developing contacts*. And then I am going to ask you to execute that strategy.

If you follow the process I'm about to share, what you'll find out is that the calls are not cold but warm. . . every single time. And you'll also find out that your lead generation (which is based on your contact generation) is significantly better than people who make traditional "cold calls." I will tell you up front that there is a potential risk in the approach I am about to share with you. It requires minimal research, and there are salespeople out there who over-research in order to *avoid* the activity of developing contacts. They don't want to make the calls. . . because they don't want to get rejected. This is known as "call avoidance," and it's based on a misunderstanding of what you're doing here. Remember, you did not go into sales in order to get approval or emotional validation.

You have the sales equivalent of a cure for cancer, and the more people you talk to, the more likely it is that someone out there will benefit from what you offer. As long as you've got that part straight, you can get a whole lot out of the next part of the book.

I'm now going to ask you to put together a solid plan for phone prospecting. The plan I am going to share is one that I began teaching after a trainee came up with his own variation on my "standard" prospecting script. This variation is so effective that I now teach it as the primary contact development plan for 90% of the salespeople I train. If you have access to the Internet, and the ability to use your own time intelligently, you can adapt this plan in your own selling environment.

Let me emphasize that a contact development plan is not the same as a calling script. Think about it: A script is something the other person has to memorize, too. If the person you are calling doesn't say what he is supposed to say, the script is useless.

A good plan, on the other hand, is more flexible.

A plan is something that an experienced general uses to define exactly what he wants to accomplish on a chaotic battlefield.

A plan is something a great chess player uses to set the strategic direction of a game.

A plan is something an entrepreneur can use to stay on track and adapt to constantly changing conditions in the marketplace.

If (or should I say "when?") something unexpected happens to the general, the chess player, or the business owner, the plan is more important than ever!

What we're going to put together over the next few chapters is a plan for a stress-free "warm call" with the person to whom you want to talk. (I'll share a plan for dealing with the gatekeeper, and for leaving voice mail messages a little bit later in the book.) Like any good plan, this one has some key objectives. As far as the initial phase of our call goes, those key objectives are:

- Minimize the stress that you and the prospect usually feel during prospecting calls. This means *not* attempting to out-talk the other person.

- Establish rapport and create a bond by disclosing information that does not necessarily seem to be in your best interests to disclose.

- Introduce yourself briefly and let the prospect know you understand the value of his time.

- Throw the prospect just a little bit off balance by seeming to hand over control of the call. That means introducing an up-front contract that allows you to explain briefly why you have called, so *the prospect can decide* whether or not to continue with the call. That way, because the prospect feels in control of the call, it's more likely that you will receive a fair hearing.

IMPORTANT: If, for some reason, you did not complete the "Internet homework" that appeared at the end of *principle 17,* make sure you have it done before you begin the next chapter. Once you've done that, it's time to refine the opening of your call.

# CHAPTER NINETEEN

## *Sandler Prospecting Principle #19: Open the Call*

Most people who write down the basics of a call opening will often create far too much text. Remember, our goal is not to outtalk or steamroll the other person. You really can open the call effectively in just a few short sentences. If you are dubious about this, read on, and I'll prove it to you. The point here is not to memorize my words but to create your own plan, one that makes sense for you and that you can deliver effortlessly.

### THE OPENING (VERSION ONE)

You: Hi, Bill, this is John Rosso. . . . I'm looking for some help—but I'm not even sure whether it makes sense for us to speak. Let me tell you the reason why I'm calling, and then you can decide whether it makes sense for us to continue. Fair?

(In case you were wondering, that's the up-front contract.)

Prospect: (Any response along the lines of "sure." If the prospect ever says that you have called at a bad time, ask when would be a better time to call back.)

You: Hey, I recently saw that (you were promoted to Senior Vice President of Everything, so congratulations on that!)

The part in parentheses, of course, reflects something you've found out ahead of time about this person and/or this company. What you reference here could be a promotion, or a paper the person wrote, or a presentation he or she gave, or even some interesting piece of news you've uncovered about the company. That parenthetical material, by the way, was the addition to the "standard" prospecting plan that made my star pupil's numbers go up so dramatically.

Important: if you have a personal connection you can reference, that trumps everything! Use that instead of online research. See *principle 27* for advice on how to open the call with the benefit of a personal connection.

For our purposes, though, let's assume you're going to do a little research on the person and/or the company. Be sure to keep what you say *brief* and focused on the individual's *professional* life. If you start talking about those embarrassing party photos of the person that you just saw on Facebook, you won't be aiding your cause!

Does this kind of opening minimize the stress on both sides? Yes! Does it establish rapport—in this case by admitting that the call might not even be necessary? Yes! Does it introduce an up-front contract that allows you to proceed with the call (if the prospect so chooses) as functional equals? Yes! Does it allow you to introduce yourself at the same time that you prove your respect for the prospect's time? Yes! Does it take the prospect just a little bit by surprise. . . by appearing to hand over control of the call? Yes!

Of course, in this particular contact development plan, you do need to make the time investment necessary to do just a little Internet lookup on the prospect. Fortunately, this is much easier and less time-consuming today than it was a few years ago. In fact, if you are willing to spring a few bucks per month for an above-average LinkedIn membership, you will usually have both a very good source for leads and something appropriate, professional, and interesting to put in between those brackets. (*NOTE*: Be sure to review the ideas in Appendix A of this book, which is all about conducting effective online searches regarding the person you're calling. These tactics can give you great information, too.)

I've already given you a couple of ideas concerning what to put between those parentheses, but the possibilities here are endless. Maybe the person was mentioned positively in some professional publication. Maybe he celebrated an anniversary with his employer. Maybe the prospect posted a video. Who knows? Between Google and LinkedIn, you can find *something* positive, and concise, and professional, to say at the outset of the call. This must be a *single concise* sentence, and it must *directly* relate to the prospect's professional life. No exceptions. This is what makes it a warm call, not a cold call.

The flattering Internet research that comes after "Actually, I'm calling because. . . " will win you valuable time, attention, and interest. . . if you do it correctly. Those few seconds will set the stage for your 30-Second Commercial, which you'll read about in the next chapter.

## THE OPENING (VERSION TWO)

What I've just shared with you is my favorite variation on the classic Sandler prospecting call. For the sake of thoroughness, here's a variation that *does not* require any up-front research but covers the same ground and attains the same basic goals:

> You: Hi, Bill, this is Jane Pierce calling from So-and-So Company. Listen, I need some help. I'm not sure if we even need to have a conversation today. Would it be okay if I briefly explain what I do and then you decide whether we should continue the conversation?

> Prospect: ("Sure" or any similar response. Again, if the prospect ever says that you have called at a bad time, ask when would be a better time to call back.)

> You: (Here you share your 30-Second Commercial, which you'll learn about in the next chapter.)

I prefer the first version I shared, but the second version has also produced great results for countless salespeople, and it may be right for you. The "right" call opening is the one that achieves all the goals *and* that you feel most comfortable delivering.

Now your job is to create your own *written* plan for opening the call. It should be just as tight, just as concise, and just as effective as the examples you've just seen. Remember, it must hit all of the opening call goals.

Create a rough-draft plan *in writing* for the opening of the call that hits *all* of the key objectives I've laid out for you:

- Minimize the stress that you and the prospect usually feel during prospecting calls. This means not attempting to outtalk the other person.
- Establish rapport by disclosing information that does not necessarily seem to be in your best interests.
- Introduce yourself briefly and let the prospect know you understand the value of his time.
- Throw the prospect a bit off balance by seeming to hand over control of the call. This means introducing an up-front contract that allows you to explain briefly why you

> **In the next chapter, you will refine your 30-Second Commercial.**

have called, so the prospect can decide whether or not to continue with the call.

# CHAPTER TWENTY

## *Sandler Prospecting Principle #20:*
## *The 30-Second Commercial*

Y ou have now created a plan for opening your telephone prospecting call. Now, let's look at what happens after the prospect agrees to hear about what you do.

The next step in the call is to present the central points of your message in a concise appeal we call the 30-Second Commercial. This is your moment in the spotlight. Make the most of it!

The 30-Second Commercial forms the heart of your prospecting call. Not only must it really, truly last no more than thirty seconds, it must describe, in a compelling way, exactly what you do and how the prospect might benefit from it.

The success or failure of your prospecting call will rely in large measure on the care with which you identify and practice the most important elements of your 30-Second Commercial. So be prepared to spend some significant time working on this. Once again, your goal is not necessarily to create a word-for-word script but rather to create a list of major bullet points you can use, practice, and internalize when it comes time to talk about the value you and your organization deliver.

Important: the objective of the 30-Second Commercial is *not to sell anything.*

Instead, it is to spark the prospect's curiosity and engage him in a conversation. The commercial should cause the prospect to wonder, "How do they do that?" Or, "Would that work in my situation?" Or, "How much would this cost?" Or any number of other similar questions.

The most successful 30-Second Commercials feature these elements:

- Introduction: the name of your company and the nature of your product or service.

- Pain statement: a brief description of your product or service from the perspective of the customers whose pains are addressed by it. You will get the best results by choosing two or three pains that are likely to be relevant to this specific prospect. Ideally, this is a plan you will be customizing to specific people and situations, not a script that you will be reciting verbatim to everyone you encounter.

- Benefit statement: a statement describing in general terms how people like your prospect have benefited from your product or service.

- Hook question: Add a question at the end that measures the relevance of your product or service to the prospect's situation. Notice that the purpose here is to "hook" the other person into a conversation, not to create a sale or any other kind of commitment. Once you create the environment for a good conversation, you can start identifying pain.

This 30-Second Commercial is likely to be the part of your contact development plan that requires the most up-front work.

This little commercial takes a maximum of 30 seconds to say, but it takes a lot longer to prepare. Think of it as a play that an NFL quarterback might call to achieve a first down. Running the play might take 30 seconds, but preparing it, practicing it, and altering it appropriately at the line of scrimmage requires a much more significant time investment.

Once you identify the elements of your commercial, it must flow naturally. **You do not have a good contact development plan if you cannot recite and revise your 30-Second Commercial at a moment's notice!**

So that is your assignment: To create and practice a 30-Second Commercial and to keep creating it and keep practicing it until you're familiar with it, comfortable with it, and don't mind changing it a little as circumstances require. I suggest you budget at least two hours to work on this extremely important element. **Notice that the 30-Second Commercial is *not* a recitation of features from your product training!**

There are many possible variations on the 30-Second Commercial, and there are numerous ways that Sandler graduates have delivered this commercial effectively. One possible template you can use looks like this:

So, Bill, I'm with (So-and-So Inc.). We're a company that specializes in (very brief description of what you do). Bill, I spend a lot of my time talking to (Vice Presidents of Everything), typically in the (manufacturing) world. And typically, when I speak to those people, here's what they say to me: They tell me their people are doing a good job of (A, B, and C), but they are *concerned* about (potential problem #1), *disappointed* with (potential problem #2), or *unhappy* with (potential problem #3). Has any of that ever been relevant to your world, or even worth a brief conversation?

Here's another template:

Bill, I'm (your name) with (name of your company). We are a (type of company) firm that specializes in (solution you deliver). We've been very successful in developing and implementing (brief description of product/service) for (companies/people) who are concerned about (potential problem #1), disappointed with (potential problem #2), or unhappy with (potential problem #3). We've been able to help our (clients/customers) to (description of product/service benefit, with the emphasis on "what's in it for me" from the customer's point of view). (NOTE: If you can include a reference to some kind of "social proof" here, such as a happy customer you've worked with, or a trade association you take part in, that's a plus.) Does anything at all of what I've just said (sound like an issue for you/seem relevant to your world/describe something with which you are dealing)?

Once you pose the hook question, you must stop talking!

If you want to use either of those templates to build your own template, you can.

If you would prefer to create a different template for yourself, one that hits the bases of *introduction, pain statement, benefit statement, and hook question*, go ahead and do that. As with the opening, what you develop must feel comfortable to you as you deliver it.

Create the bullet points for a 30-Second Commercial that include an *introduction, a pain statement, a benefit statement, and a hook question.* Practice saying it out loud. Be comfortable enough to deliver it spontaneously, without reading any of your notes. *Do not* move on to *principle #21* until you have done this.

# CHAPTER TWENTY-ONE

## *Sandler Prospecting Principle #21: No Stress (On You)*

I f you are reading these words, it should be because you are already comfortable delivering your 30-Second Commercial verbally, without looking at your notes.

It's not all that important that you deliver the commercial in exactly the same way every single time, but it *is* extremely important that you be able to deliver it while feeling OK about yourself, without putting any kind of stress on yourself. This is because the prospecting call you are about to make is built on a stress-free foundation.

This is your prospecting call. Nobody is being judged in any way here, certainly not you. You cannot "get it right" or "get it wrong." You can only relax and adopt the best practices I've shared with you.

In that spirit, let me ask you to re-examine your own 30-Second

Commercial by comparing it to the following sample commercial. Like the one you just built, it hits all the bases: It has an introduction, a pain statement, a benefit statement, and a hook question. If studying the sample below leads you to uncover something that you can improve in your own commercial, go ahead and make the change. If not, stick with what you have, because the heart of your no-stress prospecting call is already in place.

> I'm Mark Smith, from ABC Company. We are a computer application development firm specializing in custom-designed inventory management programs for manufacturing and distribution operations.
>
> We've been very successful in developing and implementing systems for companies that are concerned about the costs associated with inaccurate inventory counts, unhappy with paperwork bottlenecks that slow down the order fulfillment process, or disappointed by the amount of time it takes to reconcile purchasing, invoicing, and shipping documents.
>
> We've been able to help customers like XYZ Company substantially improve their ability to track, process, and account for inventory while eliminating redundant paperwork and speeding up the accounting process.
>
> Does anything at all of what I've just said seem relevant to you?

When you have revised your 30-Second Commercial and practiced it out loud until you feel no stress whatsoever delivering it, you are ready to move on.

Tomorrow, you will connect the dots on your Contact Development Plan.

# CHAPTER TWENTY-TWO

*Sandler Prospecting Principle #22:*
*No Stress (On the Person You're Calling)*

Once you are clear enough with your 30-Second Commercial that you can deliver it authentically, without putting stress on yourself, you are ready to follow through on a core commitment of this book. We call it the "no-stress warm call."

It's time to connect the dots on your contact development plan. Remember, this is not a cold call. The no-stress warm call is specifically designed to minimize or eliminate the stress that you and the prospect usually feel during prospecting calls.

Here's how it will play out:

You will *open* the call, using the research that you have done online to help establish rapport. Then you will create an up-front contract that puts control of the call in the hands of the prospect.

You will then *transition into your 30-Second Commercial.* If all goes well, your "hook" question will get the prospect to bite on one of the problems referred to in the commercial.

Once the prospect is hooked, you will engage him or her in a brief *conversation* to more fully develop the situation and the potential pain.

If you uncover enough pain, you will then *close* for an appointment.

You will then *post-sell by identifying any obstacles that might arise to keep the appointment from taking place.*

## THE NO-STRESS WARM CALL

- Open
  - (Mini up-front contract)
  - (Make a personal connection)
- Transition into 30-Second Commercial
- Conversation/pain
- Schedule an appointment
- Post-sell

Take a look at how it might play out in a real call. What follows is a composite of the kinds of calls Sandler alumni actually execute, day in and day out.

## OPEN

Salesperson: Hi. This is Jane Smith with Acme Media. Listen, I need some help. I'm not sure if we even need to have a conversation today. Would it be okay if I briefly explain why I'm calling and then you decide whether we should continue the conversation?

Prospect: Sure. What's up?

Salesperson: Actually, one reason I wanted to reach out was that I saw an article of yours I really enjoyed, called *The Art of Online Discounting*. I liked that piece a lot, and I really wanted to thank you for putting it out there.

Prospect: My pleasure. I didn't know anybody outside of my immediate family read that article.

## TRANSITION INTO 30-SECOND COMMERCIAL

Salesperson: Well, I wanted to let you know I saw that. In fact, I just forwarded it to my boss. Now, here's the other reason for my call. My company is Acme Media, and typically, merchandise managers like yourself work with us because they're concerned about how much money they're spending on advertising that is glitzy but doesn't increase sales. Very often, they're disappointed with the "cookie cutter" approach they get from traditional agencies. For instance, we work with companies like Big Department Store because we have the ability to define and narrowly target the right audience with digital, broadcast, and on-site exposure. We've been able to develop highly customized micro-campaigns for them. The success of those campaigns can be directly and quickly measured by increased sales and revenues in real time.

## CONVERSATION/PAIN

Salesperson: Is any of that relevant to you?

Prospect: Yeah, sure.

Salesperson: I'm curious. How often have you had that experience of investing in a campaign that looked promising but didn't meet your expectations?

Prospect: Well, I think everyone in our industry has run campaigns that underperformed. We're no exception. I know we ran one ad earlier this year for which the agency actually won an award. . . but frankly, we were disappointed by the results.

Salesperson: Interesting. Can you tell me more about that?

(The prospect elaborates, and further pain points emerge.)

Salesperson: Sounds like a frustrating situation. Can you think of a more recent example?

(The prospect gives an example that is higher in emotion.)

Salesperson: And so, because of that, what happened?

(The prospect discusses the impact of the problem.)

## SCHEDULE THE APPOINTMENT

Salesperson: May I make a suggestion?

Prospect: Sure.

Salesperson: Let's do this—pick a day to invite me in, and we can discuss this further for 30 minutes. We may have something for you; we may not. Would you be open to a conversation?

Prospect: OK. Why don't you come by on Wednesday afternoon, say three o'clock?

Salesperson: Yes. That's fine. I look forward to meeting with you.

## POST-SELL

Salesperson: And listen, before we hang up, can you think of anything that will come up between now and next Wednesday that would cause you to change or cancel the appointment?

Prospect: No. I'm putting it in my calendar as we speak.

Salesperson: OK. I'm doing the same.

One last thing—in preparation for our meeting next Wednesday, would you give some thought to the top three concerns you've got in the areas of advertising and promotion? That will be a great starting point for our discussion.

Prospect: Sure.

## THAT'S WHAT IT SOUNDS LIKE!

What you've just read is one example of what the no-stress warm call sounds like when it's delivered properly.

When we share it with salespeople, we generally get two big questions about this contact development plan. These questions concern prospects' objections ("How do you handle them?") and gatekeepers ("How do you get past them?"), respectively. You'll find them covered in *principles 23* and *24*.

> **In the next chapter, you will learn
> how to deal with gatekeepers.**

# CHAPTER TWENTY-THREE

*Sandler Prospecting Principle #23:*
*Generate a Referral from the Gatekeeper*

"What do I do if I reach a gatekeeper instead of the person I want to reach?"

This part of the call is routinely messed up by salespeople. I made a point of showing you *how* it usually gets messed up near the beginning of the book. Remember that?

If *all* you get from this book is how not to leave the stink of fear with the gatekeeper, then your time will have been well spent. You can dramatically improve your performance just by acknowledging that how you've previously handled gatekeepers probably hasn't been serving you well.

So let's change that. Most salespeople don't realize it, but when they reach a gatekeeper who happens to be the contact's personal assistant, what they are actually doing is asking for a referral. Usually, they sabotage that request for a referral by stinking up the place with fear, and/or by trying to "get around" the gatekeeper.

I speak from experience here. Before I started prospecting the Sandler way, I botched countless referral requests when I interacted with gatekeepers. I did what just about everyone else does. Take a look.

Executive assistant: Mike Bigwig's Office. This is Shannon.

By the way, that's a big tipoff that you've reached a very different type of gatekeeper than the front-desk receptionist. You hear the actual name of the contact you're trying to reach! That's a clear sign that this is the person we need to engage with for a referral! But is that what usually happens? No.

Salesperson: Hi, can I speak to Mike, please? (Or, "Mike Bigwig, please.") (Or, "Is Mike available?")

Of course, executive assistants hear variations on these openings several dozen times a week. They are almost as sick of them as you are. Is it any surprise that the call goes downhill from here? After all, this person's job is to keep the wrong people away from the boss. . . and make sure only the right people get through. The tone of your voice is enough to tell the assistant this is a sales call. Look what happens next.

Executive assistant: May I ask who's calling? (Or, "May I ask what this is regarding?")

Now you know you're in trouble, so you decide, on the spot, that you're going to get tricky.

Salesperson: It's regarding an important business matter.

Or some other piece of doubletalk. You sense, even as the doubletalk comes rushing out of your mouth, that this isn't going to work either. So, about five seconds into the call, you're already crashing and burning. What do you do? You decide to get tricky again. Quick, though. Before the gatekeeper has a chance to pose one of those annoying questions again.

> Salesperson: Shannon, can you just ask Mike to call me, please? It's John Rosso, and the number is (555)-555-5555. Do you need me to repeat that?

Wow. You've established no rapport whatsoever with this person. . . but that doesn't matter, right? Suddenly you're issuing orders. Did you notice that you're also asking for a referral to the most important person in this prospect's working life? And that you're doing that with absolutely no evidence of any potential value delivered or any respect for Shannon's role?

So what's going to happen?

I'll tell you. I know, because what you just read is what I used to do. It's one reason that my numbers were so terrible. What's going to happen next is that Shannon is going to tune you out.

Even if the executive assistant agrees to your little dictation instructions (which she might pretend to do, just to get you off the phone), your odds of getting any kind of advocacy on your behalf for a call back are slim to nonexistent. Me, I would bet on nonexistent.

If what you just read is in any way reminiscent of what you are doing now when you interact with gatekeepers, let me ask you a question, with apologies to TV's Dr. Phil: How's that working out for you?

## The Three Questions

Remember, there are three things a gatekeeper wants to know:

- "Who's calling?"
- "What's your company?"
- "Does my boss know what this is regarding?"

Hot tip: if you *answer* those questions, in order, before the gatekeeper even asks them, you'll be in good shape. But there's also a fourth priority that most salespeople ignore: whenever you reach the executive assistant, you need to assume you're talking to the decision maker and move smoothly into your warm call.

You read right. This person deserves to be treated *exactly* like your target contact.

So instead of asking for a referral cold, with no rapport and no respect, you should begin the call differently and execute it differently. Look at how well this call can go if we just change the approach and interrupt the pattern Shannon is so used to hearing.

Executive assistant: Mike Bigwig's Office. This is Shannon.

Salesperson: Hey there, Shannon. If Mike is around, would you let him know that you have John Rosso on the line?

This interrupts the conditioned response. Most salespeople do not open with this.

Executive assistant: I'm sorry. He's not available right now.

Don't assume Shannon is lying. Assume Shannon is *telling the truth!* Continue with:

Salesperson: He doesn't have voice mail, does he?

Another pattern interrupt. (By the way, if you were talking to the front-desk receptionist, this question would move you forward to voice mail nine times out of 10.)

Executive assistant: You can leave a message if you want, but I'm the one who listens to them.

Once you hear something like that, you can rest assured that you have, in fact, reached an executive assistant. What you do next is incredibly simple: Treat Shannon just the way you would treat Mike! Show Shannon the same respect, proceed with the call in the same way, and pose the same questions.

Salesperson: Oh, I see. Is it OK, then, if I let you know the reason why I'm calling?

What is she going to say? "No?" Remember, she is trying to figure out what the purpose of the call is. Nine times out of 10, you will hear this:

Executive assistant: That would be great.

Salesperson: Shannon, I've got a company called ABC Training. It's a sales management training and consulting firm. I do a lot of work with presidents and owners of companies that are in the high tech space, just like your firm. In fact, I've got a number of clients who sell directly to banks, just as you guys do.

Sound familiar? It should. This is the beginning of your 30-Second Commercial, intelligently adapted for this conversation. At the end of the commercial, of course, you will ask something like:

Salesperson: Does any of that sound relevant or worthwhile?

More often than you expect, Shannon will say, "Yes"—and will make absolutely sure you get through to the boss.

Our clients have generated more referrals from executive assistants than they can count by using this classic Sandler technique. And you can too. Just do what I've laid out here and treat the assistant with complete respect.

If you do that, you will generate the ultimate referral!

(I'll have more to share about referrals a little later on in the book... but until then, just bear in mind that this one is probably the most important one you will ever generate.)

**In the next chapter, you will learn how to deal with the obstacles you encounter during the prospecting call.**

# CHAPTER TWENTY-FOUR

## *Sandler Prospecting Principle #24: Reverses*

"How do I turn around objections?"

You don't.

A lot of prospecting "systems" out there try to give you snappy comebacks for the "common objections" you are likely to hear during a phone call. In other words, the authors of these systems try to tell you that, every time you hear an "objection" (such as, "Aren't you guys a lot more expensive than XYZ Company?"), you should have a preprogrammed "turnaround" ready. Supposedly, once you recite the magic words of your "turnaround," you will neutralize the objection and be able to pick up from where you left off in your calling script.

It doesn't work.

Not only that. We all *know* it doesn't work, because we get calls from salespeople ourselves. But for some reason, we keep trying to turn around objections with these catchy little phrases. Then we wonder why our calling numbers are so bad.

Of course, you will encounter resistance and obstacles during some of your prospecting calls. But since our goal on the prospecting call is to facilitate a conversation that eventually connects to some kind of pain that our organization can relieve, we're not going to pretend that we can "turn around" anything. Instead, we're going to deepen the conversation by using a technique called "reversing."

Reversing is a questioning strategy that will help you avoid "mind reading." The fact is when you run into an obstacle, objection, or challenge on one of these calls, you don't yet know to what anything really connects. So instead of trying to "solve" or "turn around" what you've just heard, you ask a question that helps you to get below the surface and get a clearer picture of what's really going on in this person's world.

Reversing usually means responding to the prospect's question or objection with a question. Whether or not you use a question, though, reversing puts the ball back in the prospect's court and generates subtle encouragement to provide additional information. After all, it's more important to find out *why* the prospect asked than it is to offer up the "answer" in a knee-jerk way.

For instance, if the prospect says, "Aren't you guys a lot more expensive than ABC Company?" . . . you could deepen the conversation through reversing by saying:

Good question. Why do you ask?

That is an interesting question. And you asked it because. . .?

Thank you for asking that. I'm curious: That is important to you because. . .?

I'm glad you asked that. What are you hoping I'd say?

Or (to use another example) if the prospect says, right off the bat, "This is not for us," you could continue the conversation by saying:

OK. I'm curious, though. What makes you say that?

Or if the prospect says, "We're happy with what we're already doing now," you could respond with:

OK. If you were me, what would you do now?

Notice that these are not "turnarounds" but invitations to take part in a richer conversation. There are a lot of different ways to use reversing but only one big guideline to follow as you implement this principle. The reverse must never be used to one-up the prospect. If any part of the call negatively affects your prospect's feeling of being "OK," you lose!

So remember that this is not a snappy comeback or a debate tool that allows you to "win" at someone else's expense. That goes not just for reverses but also for every aspect of the call. Don't ask questions in a way that comes off as assertive or pushy. Don't move too quickly through the call; pace your responses to the other person's speaking rhythm. If you follow these guidelines, you will find that reverses make it much easier for you to create an environment where you can identify potential pain areas.

An effective reverse will get you closer to a dialogue about the relevant pain the prospect is experiencing. Move on to *principle 25* to learn about some questions that will help you to define the extent of the prospect's perceived problem.

> ### In the next chapter, you will learn how to uncover pain during the prospecting call.

# CHAPTER TWENTY-FIVE

*Sandler Prospecting Principle #25:
The Sandler Pain Funnel*

Before you invest the time, attention, and other resources necessary to schedule a time to talk about your solution, you need to uncover pain. Ideally, your prospect needs to give you clear evidence that the appointment really does make sense for both sides. That evidence may come during this call in the form of what what we call "pain indicator statements."

These are statements from the prospect that show there really is more than just abstract "interest" in what you're talking about together but a real, live problem that has an emotional impact on your contact, right now. Once you hear a pain indicator statement, there is no excuse for not setting the appointment.

Pain indicator statements *don't* sound like this:

- "We're interested in. . ."

- "I'm supposed to gather information about. . ."
- "We're exploring the possibility of. . ."

Pain indicator statements *do* sound like this:

- "I'm not real happy about ..."
- "We need to be able to (X) by (date)."
- "I'm concerned about ..."
- "I'm disappointed with ..."
- "We should have accomplished (X) by now."

And so on. The words the prospect uses to express the problem don't matter as much as the emotion that comes across on the phone.

Although it is OK to schedule (and post-sell!) calendar appointments with people who are interested in what you offer, it is much, much better to confirm a calendar slot with someone who has shared a pain indicator statement with you. The whole point of the conversation you have with the prospect is to uncover pain that carries an emotional impact.

The Sandler Pain Funnel has been proven extremely effective at defining the emotional extent of the prospect's perceived problem. Although there are many other effective questioning strategies for uncovering pain, the Sandler Pain Funnel is an excellent place to start, and perhaps the best all-around questioning tool for those just beginning to prospect the Sandler way.

When you hear the prospect share a story or incident that seems like it *could* connect to a pain indicator statement, ask for more details. . .

- Tell me more about that.
- Can you be a bit more specific? Give me an example.
- How long has that been a problem?

- What have you tried to do about that?
- And did that work?
- How much do you think that has cost you?
- How do you feel about that?

When you hear a pain indicator statement and have gotten the prospect to share his or her feelings about it, the odds are that it is time to schedule the next discussion.

During prospecting calls, one good way to schedule the meeting might sound like this:

Salesperson: Hey, Brandon, can I make a suggestion?

Prospect: Please.

Salesperson: If you can, take a look at your calendar and let's find some time over the next two weeks where you can have the chance to invite me in. We could talk a little bit more about some of the challenges you're facing; I can discuss some of the programs we've put together for some of your counterparts at other companies. . . and my guess is that, between the two of us, we should to be able to figure out at that point whether there's something I can do to help you.

(Of course, once you do get the time and date, you will want to complete the call with a post-sell discussion. What possible obstacles to the meeting might come up? How will they be handled?)

> In the next chapter, you will learn how
> to leave effective voice mail messages.

# CHAPTER TWENTY-SIX

## *Sandler Prospecting Principle #26: Leave Voice Mail Messages*

Y ou and I live in an era in which we must overcome a major barrier that stands between ourselves and the people we want to talk to. It's called voice mail.

Usually, salespeople leave a voice mail message that sounds like this:

> "Hi, Bill, this is Brad Danforth calling from ABC Widget Company. I'm just calling to check in and see whether you've got any needs in the widget area that we might be able to discuss. If you do, please give me a call at (555)-555-5555. Bill, I hope you're having a great day, and I look forward to hearing from you. Again, the number is (555)-555-5555."

This is what we call a worst practice. We call it that because it doesn't work! This approach almost never secures a return call. It typically generates a one, two, or three percent response rate. As a result of those dismal numbers, a lot of salespeople give up on voice mail altogether. The trouble is, that's a worst practice, too. We want to leave *some* kind of message because most of the time, we don't reach the people with whom we are trying to have a conversation. So we have to say something! The question is: what do we say?

Let's face it. Voice mail is a challenge! And once we break it down, we see that there are two main varieties of voice mail challenge:

- Voice mail messages for people you have not talked to yet, and want to.
- Voice mail messages for people you already have talked to, at least once and had a good conversation with—but can't seem to get on the phone again.

Let's look at each of these separately.

In the first category are people who are on our list to call for the very first time. Maybe we've done a little research up front on this person. Maybe we're following up on a referral. It doesn't really matter how we got the name and number; we got it, and we want to develop the contact. We call the number and we hear a voice mail message urging us to leave our name, number, and a brief message.

For these people, you should:

- Keep the message short. Don't overwhelm the person with lots of information. Think of this as a *10-second* commercial. Here again, the up-front research you did makes this less of a "cold" voice mail and more of a "warm" voice mail. *Do not* leave your entire 30-Second Commercial on the person's voice mail system.

- Keep the message understandable and accessible. If you keep your message extremely simple, as outlined above, and you don't get any callbacks, it's either because your message is difficult to understand, or because your tonality is off. Record a message for yourself, then play it back for yourself, your colleagues, and your loved ones. Ask the tough questions: "Can you understand what I'm saying? How is my tonality? Would *you* call me back based on this message?" Request brutal honesty, and make any appropriate changes.

Practice leaving messages that are easier to understand and more accessible, and listen to your own "playback" sample messages regularly.

- Keep your expectations realistic. Anyone who tells you there is a system that will get *everyone* to return your messages is lying to you. What you are looking for is a steady stream of messages, left every single calling day, resulting in a steady stream of callbacks. Monitor your own numbers over time, and keep it up. If you are ever tempted to stop leaving short, direct messages because of what one particular person did or didn't do, remember what hockey great Wayne Gretzky said: "You miss 100% of the shots you don't take."

Here are two variations that show what a voice mail message following these guidelines might sound like, the first being one you can use when you *don't* have a personal connection with the prospect:

Hey, Bill. John Rosso. Listen, I'm doing a little bit of research on you and ABC Company. I saw that you published a paper recently on sustainable materials in the packaging industry. I have a couple of questions for you. Bill, call me—again, it's John Rosso, and my number is (555)-555-5555.

Click. The call is done. No hemming, no hawing, no life story. And here's a model you could follow in those situations where you *do* have a personal contact:

Hey, Bill. This is John Rosso. It's about 4:20 on Tuesday. Hey, I had a nice conversation with David Jones over at Acme Corporation. He thought it would be important that you and I talk. I promised him I would reach out to you. The number is (555)-555-5555.

Click. Again, the call is over. No please, no thank-you, nothing. Not because we don't want to be polite but because people who hear those words in a voice mail message tend to associate them with nervous salespeople and then delete the message!

These two examples are what we call best practices because they typically generate return calls in the 50 percent range, which I think you will agree is a heck of a lot better than one, two, or three percent. The other thing these messages have in common is that they each require just a little work up front, about as much time as having a good conversation with someone, or conducting a quick Internet search. Not a lot of work. A little work. By the way, if you ever find yourself spending 20 minutes "researching" a single lead you've never spoken to before, that's too much time!

Now, what about those people you *do* have at least one solid conversation with, or maybe even meet with, who then seem to fall off the face of the earth?

These disappearing acts are frustrating, I know, but they are also occupational hazards of selling for a living, so you might as well find a way to deal with the challenge effectively. One good way to deal with it is when a significant amount of time has gone by without any kind of communication with the person (and yes, "significant" varies from person to person), you can call and leave a message that sounds something like this:

> Carol, it's John Rosso from Sandler Training. Hey, I thought we had a productive meeting a couple of weeks back. However, I've left several voice mail messages and haven't heard back from you. Maybe you've been extremely busy and you have been unable to get back to me. That's understandable. Or perhaps you've decided on an approach that is different from what we discussed. If that's the case, my number is (555)-555-5555. If you could give me a quick call back, I can close the file on this for now.

That usually clarifies what's going on.

As you refine your technique, you may end up creating a whole sequence of voice mail and email messages that support and complement each other.

---

**In the next chapter, you will learn to generate and use referrals.**

# CHAPTER TWENTY-SEVEN

## Sandler Prospecting Principle #27: Generate and Use Referrals

Most salespeople are uncomfortable asking for referrals and introductions. That's because they do it wrong.

Most salespeople are so terrified of being turned down that they postpone the discussion, waiting until the last possible moment to address the issue. Typically, that's the end of the meeting or the phone conversation. Then they say something like this: "Hey, by the way, you wouldn't happen to know about anyone who might be able to benefit from working with me, would you?"

Talk about a question that's designed to get you shot down!

Nine times out of 10, the other person just says, "Gee, no, I can't. Sorry." Or, if you're really lucky, "Hmm. . . let me think about it." Both of which translate to nothing. The experience is awkward and sometimes a little humiliating, which explains why a lot of salespeople don't even make it this far. The result: they get far fewer referrals than they should.

There's a better way to do this, and it starts with understanding what salespeople really do for a living. *We save people's necks.*

As professional salespeople, we bail people out. We are solution providers. We provide tremendous insight to our clients. We change their world! We save the day, just like the cavalry coming over the hillside in those old westerns. We deliver value! So rule number one when it comes to referrals is that you have to be ready to talk about the value you have delivered. . . first! I find that a phone call is a great way to do this, and I think you will, too.

Let's assume you're called in to save the person's neck, bail the person out, solve the problem—and you do that with style.

Then you have a phone discussion (or perhaps an in-person meeting) that sounds like this:

You: So, was this project helpful to you? Did you find what we did here valuable?

Client: Yes, it has definitely helped us a lot. (Or some similar response.)

Then, instead of "by the way," which puts you in an "inferior" position, you continue with:

You: You know, I'd like to talk to you about something that could have a significant impact, if you have a minute.

(Put all this in your own words.)

Client: Sure.

(Next, you tell a disarmingly honest story. It could sound like the below.)

You: Jim, how long have you and I worked together? Four years? Wow. I've always felt we've got a good relationship, and I've also felt that you've seen value in what we do. Is that a fair statement?

Client: Absolutely.

You: I will tell you, every time I leave here, I kick myself. I keep thinking I'd like to have a conversation with you about people in your circle, who would be open to understanding more about what we do. But I've just never brought it up. In my head, I always thought. . . . I didn't want to come across too "salesy" or look as if I was imposing.

(That's a disarming piece of honesty!)

You: Would it be helpful if I painted a picture of the 3 to 4 kinds of people who typically are a good fit for what we do?

Prospect: Sure.

You: Let's just brainstorm together who you are connected to that fits the profile—then you and I can decide later if it makes sense to make an introduction. Sound okay?

Now, how much more effective is that than, "Hey, by the way, you wouldn't happen to know about anyone who might be able to benefit from working with me, would you?" Way more effective, right?

I'll tell you what's going to happen next. Your client is going to give you the names and phone numbers of one or more people to call and more than likely provide a warm introduction.

## GENERATING THE REFERRAL: VOICE MAIL

What's the conversation going to sound like when you do reach out to Joe, the person Jim referred to you? There are a couple of different scenarios to consider. We'll begin by assuming that you're attempting to connect with Joe by phone, which is what I recommend, even if you happen to already have some kind of social media connection to Joe. You might be one of the 500 people following Joe on Twitter, but the odds are pretty good that you have not yet won what the marketing people call "top of mind awareness" with him. For that, you need a conversation.

And the good news about this particular conversation is that, although it has many variations, all of them are built around what we call a "warm introduction," and all of them use that introduction to segue into the basic prospecting conversation I've outlined for you in this book.

Let's take a look at some of the variations you can use. The most common variation is the voice mail message, because these days, it's very unlikely that you'll reach anybody voice to voice on the first call. So here are three more options for leaving initial messages when you have a personal connection with the person you're calling. Notice once again that each message is very short!

> You: Hey, Joe. John Rosso. Listen, I had a real good conversation with Jim Smith yesterday. We had a chance to talk a little bit about you and your business. He thought it might be important that you and I speak. I'm at (555)-555-5555.

Or:

> You: Hey, Joe. I had a conversation with Jim Smith yesterday, and he talked to me a little bit about you and your

business. He thought it might be important that you and I speak briefly. I promised him I would reach out to you. I'm at (555)-555-5555.

Or even, if you want to add a little humor:

You: Hey, Joe. I talked recently to Jim Smith. If he's still someone you'd even consider admitting that you know publicly, then you should also know that he and I had a very good conversation about you and your business yesterday. He thought it might be important that you and I speak briefly. I promised him I would reach out to you. I'm at (555)-555-5555. Give me a call.

## GENERATING THE REFERRAL: VOICE TO VOICE

When Joe calls us back, or if we get Joe on the phone voice to voice the first time we call, we're not going to say what we normally would say if we were initiating contact with someone who has no referral-network connection to us. The dynamic is a little different here. This time we're going to say something like this:

You: Hey, Joe. John Rosso.

Then, believe it or not, right after we say our name, we're going to let a precious second or two go by: tick, tick, tick. No words come out for those first two seconds or so of the call. Now, I realize that that may feel counterintuitive because we salespeople have a tendency to want to fill every available empty space during our conversations. But watch what happens right after this little pause.

You: Is that name at all familiar to you?

Prospect: Nope.

You: OK, I was hoping it would be. Hey, I had a nice conversation with Jim Smith the other day about your business.

A couple of things can happen at this point. The prospect might say, "Jim Smith, sure, go on" or any variation that translates as, "Keep talking," in which case we're off to the races, ready to have an exchange about why Jim felt it made sense for us to have a discussion.

Or the prospect can say nothing or can say, "Jim who?" or can say anything else that translates as "I don't know what the heck you're talking about." If that happens, don't panic. This is our way forward:

You: Hmm, it doesn't sound like you and he talked recently.

Prospect: (Any response.)

You: Listen, not a problem. Let me share with you the conversation Jim and I had, why he thought it might be important that you and I speak, and then you can tell me whether or not it makes sense for the two of us to sit down together. Fair?

And from there on in the call is the same as a standard prospecting call.

Did you notice that there is no point in this call at which we use the word "referral" to the prospect? Let me tell you why that is. Words are funny things; if you use the wrong one, even innocently, you can set off all kinds of alarm bells within the other person's defense systems. A prospect might think, "*Referral*? Somebody *referred* me? That means I'm eventually supposed to buy something, right? Abort! Abort!" (Or even worse—"I got your name from...")

Somewhere along the way, the word "referral" picked up a lot of baggage. It reminds people of pushy insurance agents and pushy lead generation programs from years gone by. Nobody can blame people for feeling hesitant about taking part in anything that seems even vaguely like it's part of someone's "referral generation" process. Most of us have just had too many bad experiences with that.

True story: There's a major insurance company that has its agents fill out their customers' applications side by side with them. As part of the completion of the application, the salesperson is supposed to ask the new customer for the names of "three friends or family members I can call" and then keep staring at the application form, with pen to paper, until the new customer supplies the names! The form literally says, "Put your pen to the paper, and do not look up until the customer speaks!"

Can you imagine the discomfort and the awkwardness of that moment. . . for both sides? I guess you're supposed to be peeking up through your eyelashes to see if the customer is moving or not.

That's horrible. That kind of selling—if you can even call it selling—is the reason why there's a crazy dysfunctional culture out there between seller and buyer. So if you're like me, if you think that there's got to be a better way to do this, an adult-to-adult way to get equal business stature, protect everyone's dignity, and still generate good leads. . . well, you're right. There is. And I've just shared it with you. That's what *Prospect the Sandler Way* is all about: how to sell without selling your dignity.

**In the next chapter, you will set up your prospecting plan.**

# CHAPTER TWENTY-EIGHT

## *Sandler Prospecting Principle #28: The Prospecting Plan*

It's time to set some goals. . . and start taking the steps that will bring you closer to those goals. Your time frame is the next *six months*, starting on your very next working day. Don't create any excuses. Build the plan!

Fill in each of the blanks below with your *best guess* as to what the right numerical targets are for you in each instance. Don't worry about nailing down the numbers with complete mathematical precision. Give this your best rough guess. You can go back, do a reality check, and fine-tune things later. For now, though, your goal is to avoid the dreaded "paralysis of analysis" problem. You will do this by *quickly* jotting down the numbers that feel most realistic to you in each of the blanks below.

Revenue goal from new clients for the next six months:

_____

New clients I want to generate:

_____

Total appointments necessary to close that many new clients:

_____

First appointments that support that number of total appointments:

_____

Contacts necessary to generate that number of first appointments:

_____

Leads I will need to generate those contacts:

_____

Fill in the blanks!

Then show your numbers to your manager, partner, or trusted colleague. Conduct a reality check. Tweak. Revise. Refine.

Then, post the final plan where you can see it every day—and get to work!

> **In the next chapter, you will learn about one of the biggest obstacles to executing the plan.**

# CHAPTER TWENTY-NINE

*Sandler Prospecting Principle #29:*
*Just Make the Calls*

S ome people in the sales community talk a lot about our
having entered a brave new sales world in the past few
years. Why? Because we now have access to social media
tools like LinkedIn, Facebook, Google+ and Twitter. According
to these people, old-fashioned prospecting, what we've been talking about in this book, is now more or less obsolete because all we
really need to be focused on is "engaging" our customers—or is
that "followers?"—in day-to-day *virtual* conversations that interest them. If we only do that, all our leads will materialize, on their
own, via the Internet. Posting updates, sending out digital polls,
announcing contests. . . . Supposedly, these are the "silver bullets"
of 21st century prospecting. They fill our pipeline with leads and
create a steady stream of "engaged" new prospects to whom we
can talk.

I obviously don't subscribe to this school of thought. Since social media tools have become such a big part of the discussion for salespeople, though, it seems appropriate to explain exactly why I disagree with this point of view and also to share some thoughts on how interactive media tools can be used intelligently as part of your sales process.

Let's acknowledge first that social media is an important part of the "warm" call technique I have shared with you here. Let's acknowledge, too, that it's not the Second Coming for sales. Back when salespeople were knocking on doors in the 1930s, and the telephone started to come into the mainstream as a business application, there were probably people who said, "Wow, this new technology is going to make selling really easy. All I have to do is pick up the phone!" New technology certainly creates new opportunities, but it doesn't change the basic dynamic. We still have to connect with people one-on-one, and we still have to work our way through the stages of the process together.

Social media's a wonderful tool, and, yes, it needs to be incorporated into your prospecting efforts, but we should never mistakenly believe that it replaces one-on-one communication. It is another tool to help you facilitate finding ways to have the conversation. . . person to person. You cannot work your way through the submarine digitally! At some point there has to be a face-to-face or voice-to-voice conversation.

Once we have acknowledged that much, as a kind of reality check, we can acknowledge that, sure, Facebook is a great place to get insights, evaluate suggestions, and start discussions. Twitter is, potentially, at least, a great news feed for you and your organization, one that can tell you a whole lot about what's working (and not working!) for your customers. And LinkedIn, properly used, can tell you various things about your own personal network's referral potential and about the relationships in place at a company to which you're trying to sell. But once someone "opts in" to our world on one of these channels, once someone raises a hand and says, "Yes, I'll be part of this discussion with you," it is still our responsibility as professional salespeople to build the relationship!

So, yes, these tools have some incredible applications at the front end of the lead generation process, and they may make some of our previously "cold" discussions a lot warmer, but they don't change the fundamentals of our job description. We still have to start that person-to-person discussion!

(See also Appendix B, *Harvesting Referrals from LinkedIn*.)

Just make the calls! Put this principle into practice *today* by making the number of "warm calls" that support your plan.

**In the next chapter, you will learn about the payoff to all that you've done in this book.**

# CHAPTER THIRTY

## *Sandler Prospecting Principle #30: Collect the Payoff*

By this point, you've learned—and implemented—29 principles that support *Prospect the Sandler Way*. Now comes the payoff.

Your most obvious payoff is more, better qualified, and higher-value prospects. However, that's not the only payoff.

There is an even bigger payoff, something of potentially much greater significance to your career: the ability to work through the different steps of the sale with the prospect. . . as a peer, an equal, and as someone who has a right to be there.

I've already mentioned one of the most important lessons David Sandler ever shared with me: The relationship you develop with your prospect is not the place to try to get your emotional needs met. That's a particularly important principle to master in the prospecting phase of the relationship, but it is relevant to every interaction you have with every lead, every prospect, and every customer. I hope this book has helped you to build that way of looking at selling into everything you do.

You not only have a right to talk to people about the value you deliver, but you have an obligation to do that. The responsibility for creating and maintaining a peer-to-peer atmosphere, an atmosphere that allows you to create and support harmonious business relationships, is yours. I hope I have given you some viable tools that will help you to fulfill that responsibility.

If you practice the principles I've shared with you, if you build them into your every discussion, if you make them part of how you think and who you are, then you will be better positioned to master the lifelong lesson of interacting with your prospects with perfect confidence, no matter what bumps in the road you encounter along the way. You deserve that, and so do they.

I hope this has been helpful for you. I'll close with the same advice David Sandler shared with me years ago: *Do the behaviors! Do the behaviors! Do the behaviors!* Resolve to remain proactive, to keep making conscious choices and performing the actions that will move you forward.

# APPENDIX A

## *Three Tips for Effective Online Searches*

S earch engine strategy is now a must for any effective prospecting campaign. Below are three tips that can make your pre-call research more productive and effective. On all of the advice below, I'm assuming you're using Google, which is what I use.

1. Use quotation marks. For example, if you're calling John Smith, VP of Operations of ABC Technologies Company, you will want to enter this text into Google: "John Smith" and "ABC Company" in quotes, because if you don't, you're probably going to get a whole lot of John Smiths, as well as some study guides about the life and times of Pocahontas. This one step can save you a significant amount of time!

2. Use Google to search only one specific site. How? Just enter this text into Google:

**site: ABCTechnologies.com "John Smith"**

Assuming that John Smith works for ABC Technologies, the text above will show you every time that "John Smith" shows up on ABC's internal Web site, ABCTechnologies.com. This is a great way to unearth information that allows you to say things like, "I see you gave a talk on reducing down time in the widget industry" or, "I see you were recently promoted." You may also want to try this text:

**site: LinkedIn.com "John Smith"**

That will, in all likelihood, point you toward John Smith's LinkedIn page, which is usually worth looking at before you make a call.

3.   Search for a PDF file. Type this into Google:

**filetype:pdf "John Smith" "ABC Technololgies"**

You will get every PDF document Google can find that references both John Smith and ABC Technologies. This can be extremely helpful when you are searching for a paper that someone has authored or trying to identify someone's activity within a professional association. Both of these tend to be recorded on PDFs. Note that, when you conduct this search on Google, *only* PDF files will show up!

Let me share one more important note on Google searches. Google's Search Tools option, which you can find using Google itself, gives you the option to adjust the time frame you're examining on any search. So if you are interested in seeing only the PDFs that have shown up with John Smith's name on them in the past week, you can do that, too.

# APPENDIX B

## *Harvesting Referrals via LinkedIn*

So let's assume you, Bill Jones, are one of my first-degree LinkedIn contacts, and I see that you're directly connected to John Smith, to whom I want to be connected as well.

What do I do? I send you an email—not a LinkedIn message, since those are more likely to be ignored—but a regular email message that says something like the following:

> Hey there, Bill, I happened to notice on your LinkedIn profile that you're connected to David Smith over at Acme Corporation. How well do you know him? Would you be willing to introduce me?

Typically, you will reply with something like this:

> Sure. I know David very well. He and I went to college together. I'd be happy to introduce you.

My return email to your message will say:

> Bill, I got your message. I really appreciate that. My experience is that an email introduction can work very well for everybody involved. I have attached a template for your review. Please feel free to edit and change it in any way you want.

The template I attach will look like this:

> David, this is John. I wanted to take the opportunity to introduce the two of you. David is a good friend of mine, and John is a sales training specialist who is engaged with a number of my clients and who does top-notch work. John, I would ask you reach out to Dave and set up a time to speak. If either of you want me to be part of that conversation, or have any questions, please reach out.
>
> All the best,
>
> Bill

Assuming you approve of my proposed message, or something like it, you will then send the message out to me and to Dave. Then I will send an email in response:

> Hey, Bill, thanks so much for the introduction. Dave, I'm really looking forward to speaking with you. I'm out of the office on Monday, Tuesday, and Wednesday of this week, but I will be back in on Thursday. I will reach out to you by phone then. What's the best number to use?

I've just set up a phone appointment!

Remember that the whole principle that makes networking on LinkedIn work is having some kind of actual person-to-person communication with your first-degree contacts! If I've never had any interaction at all with you before I reach out to you about Dave Smith, the technique I've just outlined probably won't work. Don't try to extend this kind of appeal to someone with whom you really have no contact or experience.

# APPENDIX C

## *Classic Pain Questions*

P ain questions can help you define the extent of the prospect's perceived problem. Some good initial pain questions include:

- Tell me more about that.
- Can you be a bit more specific? Give me an example.
- How long has that been a problem?
- What have you tried to do about that?
- How do you feel about that?
- Have you given up trying to deal with the problem?

You may also want to ask questions that focus on a facet of your product or service that addresses some aspect of the prospect's existing or potential problem, or provides a benefit the prospect is not currently receiving. For instance:

- If there was one thing you'd like to see improved in your existing _____, what would that be?
- What would be the long-term benefit of (streamlining/consolidating/expanding) your _____ process?
- What impact would there be on (profits/production/revenues/expenses) if you could _____?
- What value would there be if it were easier to _____?
- How significant a benefit would it be if you could reduce the manpower needed to _____?
- What would be the impact of increasing the effectiveness of _____?
- Being able to speed up the _____ process would allow you to do what?
- What reasons might you have for reducing the time it takes to _____?
- How important would it be to reduce the cost of your _____?
- What would you be able to accomplish if you were able to _____?
- If you wanted to _____, how difficult might it be?
- If you needed to _____, what obstacles would you encounter?
- What would prevent you from improving _____?
- If it were necessary to _____, what would be the biggest challenge?
- If _____ didn't improve, how concerned would you be?

# ABOUT THE AUTHOR

**JOHN ROSSO** plays an important role in Sandler's worldwide organization, and is recognized nationally and internationally as a business development expert specializing in executive sales consulting and sales productivity training. A dynamic, enthusiastic speaker certified in the proprietary selling system developed by David H. Sandler, John informs, entertains, and motivates leadership and rank-and-file sales teams to achieve at their full potential.

John's authentic, real-world approach to the sales process speaks to visionary business and sales professionals who want the freedom that success brings. By leveraging over two decades of Sandler experience, and by focusing on buyers' and sellers' attitudes and behaviors, not just their techniques, John's clients achieve superior selling results.

Specifically, John focuses on helping people succeed by transforming attitude (via the principle that 90% of success resides between the ears), behavior (what daily accountabilities lead to success?) and techniques (what should be said or done at each individual step of the sales process to produce a positive outcome?). John has been a Sandler® trainer since 1994.

# CONGRATULATIONS!

## *Prospect*
## *The Sandler Way*
### *includes a complimentary seminar!*

Take this opportunity to personally experience the non-traditional sales training and reinforcement coaching that has been recognized internationally for decades.

Companies in the Fortune 1000 as well as thousands of small-to medium-sized businesses choose Sandler Training for sales, leadership, management, and a wealth of other skill-building programs. Now, it's your turn, and it's free!

You'll learn the latest practical, tactical, feet-in-the-street sales methods directly from your neighborhood Sandler trainers! They're knowledgeable, friendly, and informed about your local selling environment.

Here's how you redeem YOUR FREE SEMINAR invitation.

1. Go to www.Sandler.com and click on the LOCATE A TRAINING CENTER button (upper right corner).
2. Select your location from the drop-down menus.
3. Review the list of all the Sandler trainers in your area.
4. Call your local Sandler trainer, mention *Prospect The Sandler Way,* and reserve your place at the next seminar!